A Journey toward Home

Soul Travel from Advent to Lent

A Mustard Seed Associates Publication

© **Mustard Seed Associates**
P.O. Box 45867
Seattle, WA 98145
website: http://msaimagine.org
blog: http://godspace-msa.com
email: mail@msaimagine.org

Unless otherwise noted, quotations are taken from THE HOLY BIBLE: NEW INTERNATIONAL VERSION®. NIV®. Copyright © 1973, 1978, 1984 by Biblica.® Used by permission of B Biblica.® All rights reserved worldwide.

Scripture quotations marked TNIV are taken from THE HOLY BIBLE, TODAY'S NEW INTERNATIONAL VERSION®. Copyright © 2001, 2005 by Biblica.® Used by permission of Biblica.® All rights reserved worldwide. "TNIV" and "Today's New International Version" are trademarks registered in the United States Patent and Trademark Office by Biblica.® Use of either trademark requires the permission of Biblica.®

Scripture quotations marked NLT are taken from THE HOLY BIBLE, NEW LIVING TRANSLATION®. Copyright © 1996, 2004. Used by permission of Tyndale House Publishers, Wheaton, IL 60189. All rights reserved.

Scripture quotations marked Phillips are taken from THE NEW TESTAMENT IN MODERN ENGLISH®. Copyright © 1962. Used by permission of HarperCollins.

ISBN: 978-0692315217

Cover Credits and Interior Design: Kristin Carroccino
O Antiphon Icon Designs: Danielle Poland
Images on the "Gather, Feast, Create" pages are from Tacuinum Sanitatis a medieval handbook on health and well-being based on the Taqwim al-sihha, an eleventh-century Arab medical treatise by Ibn Butlan of Baghdad Any clipart or other artwork not specifically credited is part of the public domain.

To all who walk with us on this journey of faith—encouraging, nurturing, and guiding our steps

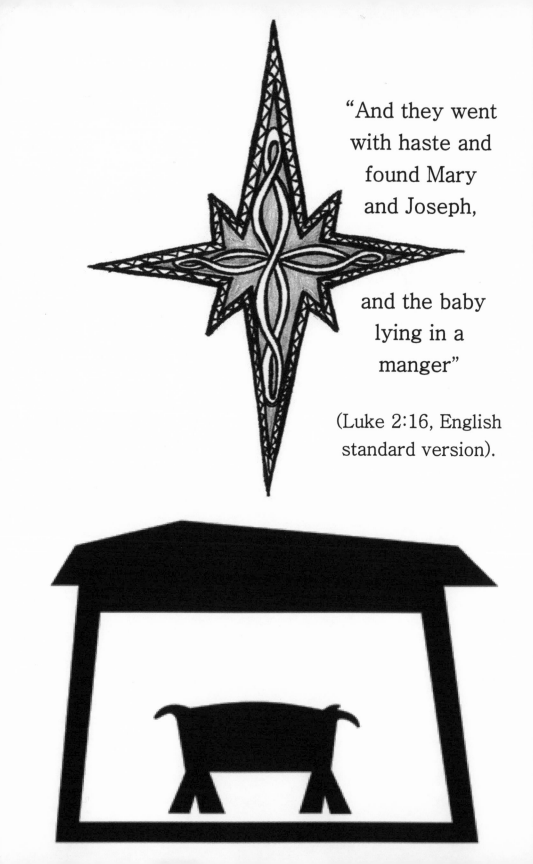

"And they went with haste and found Mary and Joseph,

and the baby lying in a manger"

(Luke 2:16, English standard version).

Contents

Collage and photo by Kristin Carroccino with assistance from Michael Carroccino and Jen Loser

Advent Liturgical Banner by Lois Prahlow via
pickandprintgallery.wordpress.com

Introduction

My six-year-old daughter is nervous. Tonight is her first time to "acolyte" at our church. Acolytes, by definition, are people who assist in the ceremonial duties of a church service, and my daughter has been excited for this moment for several months. Tonight she has uncharacteristically pulled her usually wild, curly hair into a neat ponytail; she is taking this job quite seriously. And tonight is no ordinary night. Advent started today, and our church has a long tradition of holding an "O Antiphon" service to begin the season.[1] The nave is hushed and dim; the pews are overfull. My son and I slide into an open space next to a friend, and I draw in a slow, deep breath and wonder how his sister will feel when she walks into this cavernous room and sees how many people have gathered. We all wait.

In an instant, the dissonant chords of "O Come, O Come Emmanuel" burst forth from the grand Flentrop organ in the balcony and roll over us, inviting us to rise. The priest reads solemn verses while spectral plumes of incense rise from a giant platter on the altar toward the heavens. Choirs sing, and between each verse of the ancient hymn, acolytes make their way to the altar. Some carry tall banners bearing ancient symbols and place them in stands behind the altar. Others, like my daughter, carry candles. Her face is set toward her destination. She is the smallest of them all, and people murmur as she glides down the aisle and places the end of the torch taller than she is into its designated spot. I breathe a sigh of relief and happiness for her. She has chosen to begin this ministry on an evening we won't forget, a night that is dark and expectant, drawing us into the beginning of a new church year and pointing toward the birth of Jesus, the Christ.

The seasons of the church year calendar surrounding Christmas are a rich time that ebb and flow between the contemplation of the miracle of Jesus' incarnation and anticipation of the joyful celebration of his birth in a stable over two thousand years ago. Christians through millennia have developed diverse practices for trying to capture the Divine Mystery that inhabits the weeks of Advent leading to the twelve days of Christmas and then flows exuberantly over into the season that begins with Epiphany. One of these practices developed by unknown author(s) sometime during the first century, and in wide use by the eighth is the prayerful singing of the O Antiphons in the last week of Advent, ending on Christmas Eve. These messianic verses primarily derived from Old Testament

---

[1] Please see Peter Hallock's article in Appendix B for more about this service.

prophesies by Isaiah are most familiar to modern ears in the verses of one of our oldest hymns "O Come, O Come Emmanuel." These sacred phrases were originally sung in ancient monasteries by two choirs alternating the chanting of the short verses (or *antiphons*) during the evening worship services of the last seven nights of Advent.

Each of the O Antiphons expresses a unique characteristic of the Messiah and refers to a biblical prophecy of his coming: O Sapientia (O Wisdom), O Adonai (O Lord), O Radix Jesse (O Root of Jesse), O Clavis David (O Key of David), O Oriens (O Rising Sun), O Rex Gentium (O King of the Nations), and O Emmanuel. Some scholars have noted that the first letter of invocation in each antiphon may be taken to form an acrostic in reverse: ERO CRAS, the response of Jesus to his people, translated "Tomorrow I will be there."

The O Antiphons are pointing the way to Bethlehem, to that place where God came down and dwelt among us. They are also pointing to The Way, the Christ, who came and still comes and is coming to redeem the whole of creation, from the lowliest caterpillar, to the hardened criminal, to the laughing, raucous child at the neighborhood playground. These ancient verses, ultimately, are prayers, fervent pleas for Jesus to come to us, in full humanity to every creature.

In *A Journey toward Home: Soul Travel from Advent to Lent,* words ancient and new, stories for the young and old engage us in this annual unfolding of miracles and mystery. We approach the rich seasons of Advent to Lent playfully, yet with yearning and determination. We seek, each year, to understand a little better The Way to which the prophets, shepherds, saints, monastic orders, the Holy Family, wise men and others pointed. Borrowing phrases from the O Antiphons, we are all on the way to Bethlehem to find the One who is the Lord, the King of Nations, the Root of Jesse, God-with-Us, the Key of David, the Radiant Dawn, and Wisdom. Let us prepare well for the journey. Along this road, often curvy and rocky, we will follow the guides of the O Antiphons as well as twenty-first century poets, writers and contributors to the *Godspace* blog, who offer their own interpretations of what it means to be waiting for Christ to come again into our hearts and be born, and thus, to save the world.

—Kristin

Once we've prepared, and embarked upon the annual journey leading to a full celebration of all twelve days of Christmas and the season of Epiphany that follows, where do we gather and with whom do we gather? For most of us, the birth of Christ conjures up images of a dirty stable where Jesus and his family are alone and abandoned. As Christmas approaches we imagine the Holy Family,

2

together with a few other outsiders—shepherds, foreigners, and animals. Maybe a glowing angel and star overhead, but who else might have been present?

According to New Testament theologian Kenneth Bailey in his wonderful book *Jesus through Middle Eastern Eyes*, **it is probable that there would have been a lot of other people enjoying the celebration, too**. Middle Eastern cultures are known for their hospitality, and Joseph was coming home with a new wife and an expected first child. The whole family would have gathered—aunts and uncles, cousins, and brothers and sisters. All of them had come home for a huge family reunion, hoping to see the new bride and the new baby. Yes, there was a Roman census that brought them together, but in a fun-loving culture like this, it would not have diminished the welcome or the excitement of a homecoming gathering. The expectation of a baby to be born in their midst would only have increased the excitement.

Jesus was probably born in the midst of busy family life. The guest room was bulging at the seams, and the only place for Joseph and his family to stay was in the main room of the house. As Bailey explains, the Greek word (**katalyma** or **kataluma**) translated as **inn** in Luke 2:7 does not mean a commercial building with rooms for travelers. It's a guest space, typically the upper room of a common village home. A simple village home in the time of King David, up until the Second World War, in the Holy Land, had two rooms—one for guests, one for the family. The family room had an area, usually about four feet lower, for the family donkey, the family cow, and two or three sheep. They are brought in last thing at night and taken out and tied up in the courtyard first thing in the morning. Out of the stone floor of the living room, close to family animals, you dig mangers or make a small one out of wood for sheep. Jesus is clearly welcomed into a family home.[2]

It was to this simple village home that both shepherds and wise men came. Shepherds, despised and regarded as unclean by their society, are visited by angels and invited to join the great homecoming celebration that marks the coming of the child who will become the Messiah. That they were welcomed and not turned away from this home is remarkable. This is good news indeed for the outcast and the despised.

Then the wise men came, according to Bailey, rich men on camels, probably from Arabia. And they came not to the city of Jerusalem where the Jews thought God's glory would shine, but to the child born in a manger around whom there was

---

[2] Kenneth E. Bailey, *Jesus Through Middle Eastern Eyes: Cultural Studies in the Gospels*, (Downers Grove, Illinois, IVP Academic 2008), 33.

already a great light. Their welcome is remarkable. They are foreigners, gentiles, unclean in the eyes of the Jews yet they are welcomed. Around the manger, in the midst of a family reunion, they find a new home, a new place of belonging that has beckoned to them across the world. This is good news for people of all nations who long for a place to call home.

Bailey tells us that the birth stories of Jesus "de-Zionize" the Messianic traditions. Hopes and expectations for the city of Jerusalem are fulfilled in the birth of the child Jesus, and they are fulfilled not just for the Jews, but for all people.[3] The new family, the community that will be formed around this child, does not look to the earthly Jerusalem as its home, but to the heavenly Jerusalem that will come down from heaven as a gift of God at the end of history (Revelation 21:1-4). And it is to this home, a place with no more tears, or oppression or starvation that all of us are beckoned by Christ's birth.

I love this imagery. Even in the birth of Jesus, we are called toward a new family and a new home. There are family and friends and animals, special visitations by angels for the despised and rejected, and a star to guide strangers and foreingers. The new family and the home envisioned in the birth of Jesus are inclusive of all who accept God's invitation.

Being playful with our imaginations and considering this version of the Christmas story, who else besides Jesus' extended family might we be leaving out of the birth scene? More importantly, who do we leave out today, as Jesus comes faithfully and eternally into our hearts and homes? This year, let us make more room in our souls, neighborhoods, and places of worship for those we have previously neglected to include in our Christmas journeys and festivities.

Which home do you imagine this year? Who is there? Whom will you welcome?

—Christine

---

[3] Bailey, 54.

How to use this Guide.

A Journey toward Home is designed to guide your journey through the seasons of Advent to Lent individually or in a small group of family or friends. The book is divided by weeks beginning with the week before Advent and ending with Christmas Eve. Starting with December 25, you will find the full celebration of all twelve days of Christmas, followed by selections and suggestions for the time between Epiphany (January 6) and Mardi Gras (the night before Ash Wednesday).

One of the O Antiphons[4] followed by a short meditation by Kristin or Christine will introduce each week or season. On Sunday through Friday, contributors from several different countries, various church affiliations, and many perspectives have generously offered their writing about where they have found Christ during Advent, Christmas, and Epiphany. On Saturdays and special holy days (traditionally called "feast days"), you are invited to "Gather, Feast, Create." Suggestions are provided for meals and activities and prayers to share with fellow travelers. At the end of the book, you will find Appendices with recipes from *A Journey toward Home's* contributors and further suggestions[5] for ways to celebrate these weeks, where we are at times filled with mystery and awe, confused, joyful, melancholy, too busy, too alone, but always seeking to know more fully the Christ born in Bethlehem.

—Kristin

---

[4] We have taken liberty with the traditional ordering of the antiphons. In some church traditions, it is customary to sing one Antiphon per night for seven nights and in a certain order; in this guide, you will find one Antiphon per week or section. Please refer to Appendix B for more detailed information about the O Antiphons.

[5] A free resource guide of ideas for observing the seasons of Advent to Lent is available at msaimagine.org under the "Resources" tab.

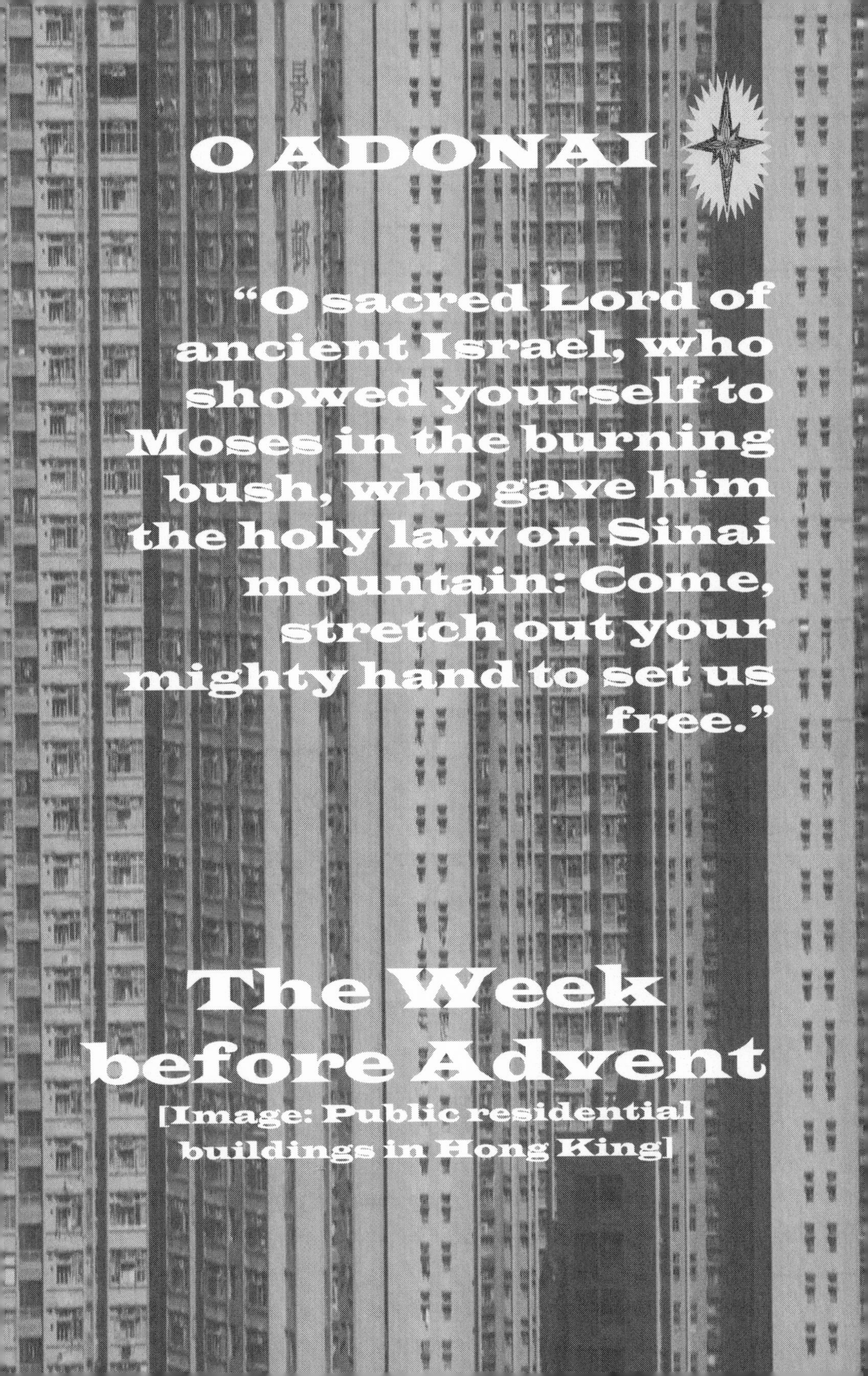

O ADONAI

"O sacred Lord of ancient Israel, who showed yourself to Moses in the burning bush, who gave him the holy law on Sinai mountain: Come, stretch out your mighty hand to set us free."

The Week before Advent

[Image: Public residential buildings in Hong King]

O Lord

The week leading up to Advent is typically a busy one. In the United States, the feast of Thanksgiving sometimes falls just a couple of days before Advent begins, and in the blink of an eye we shift from gathering with our communities and sharing rich meals and prayers of gratitude to the season that ultimately leads to Christmas. In our home, where we are raising two young children, we have usually spent the month of November building a "thankful tree," in which paper leaves cut from autumnal shades of construction paper are filled out each evening by each of us, as well as any friends who may be visiting, and stuck to the wall near a large paper tree with some tape or putty, either on a branch or sometimes several feet away, as if a sudden gust of wind had loosened the leaf and cast it astray. By the first day of Advent, the wall is full of thankful leaves, and we feel ready to begin counting the days to Christmas.

And if we have planned well, we will be digging in the attic for the metal Advent wreath form, our wooden Advent calendar, and our collection of pictures of Mary and the Holy Family that we display alongside. This is the week that we prepare for the new church year[6] and prepare to wait during Advent for the arrival of the Christ. Like Moses before the burning bush in this week's Antiphon, we stand on Holy ground and prepare room in our hearts to receive the mystery of the upcoming season by offering thanksgiving, gathering ideas, and resources. We seek to maintain the tension of contemplation and exuberant joy. We get out our calendars and plan and schedule intentionally our time over the next weeks, remembering the gradual building of anticipation of Advent that bursts into celebration for the twelve days of Christmas followed by the aptly named season of "Epiphany," when we make time to read the stories of Jesus' new ministry and mark time by being open to our own new revelations, discoveries, epiphanies.

In all of the days that unfurl before us as we contemplate Christmas gift lists and cards and recipes for feasts, charitable deeds, the wonderment of children, the quiet chill of the Northern winter or building heat of the Southern hemisphere, loneliness or overwhelm, we pray to Adonai, "come stretch out your mighty hand to set us free." Albert Camus said, "The only way to deal with an unfree world is to become so absolutely free that your very existence is an act of rebellion." In this week of preparing for Advent to Lent, we aim in our

---

[6] In the church calendar year, contrasted to the civic calendar, the beginning of the year is Advent. Writer Corean Bakke says, "The church year is grounded in ancient time and place, repeated every year. The seasons – Advent, Christmas, Epiphany, Lent, Easter, and Pentecost – are like chapters in the story." Corean Bakke, *Practicing the Church Year: A Spirituality for the Home* (Acme: Corean Bakke, 2012), 7.

waiting for Christ's arrival to cast off those parts of ourselves that hinder peace, joy, and gratitude, so that we may find freedom.

—Kristin

Prayer for the Week before Advent

God eternal, righteous and glorious One,
We give you thanks.

For your breath that fills us with life,
for love that softens our hearts,
for beauty revealed at every turn,
Christ redeemer, faithful and forgiving One,
we give you thanks.

For renewal, transforming our lives,
for peace calming the chaos of our souls,
for hope restoring our faith,
Spirit sustainer, abiding and compassionate One,
We give you thanks.

For caring when our hearts are aching,
for friends supportive in times of need,
for generosity, lavish and overflowing,
Triune God,
Eternal One, Redeeming One, Sustaining One,
We give you thanks.

For you.

—Christine

SUNDAY. Preparing for Advent.
Corean Bakke.

A small pottery piece with a pregnant Mary riding sidesaddle on a donkey led by Joseph is placed on the fireplace mantel along with candles in blue, purple, and pink. The closing portion of a poem by Tim Bascom, "Waiting for Gabriel," adds a written commentary to the mantel. A bell pull made of Norwegian Hardanger lace hangs from one end, temporarily replacing the bell kept there to announce meals.

My collection of blue dishes comes down from the high cupboard and moves into the cupboard nearest the kitchen table. A collection it is. Few pieces match. Many shades of blue are involved. It includes two small Mexican bowls decorated with deep blue flowers, and two smaller light-blue porcelain bowls purchased in Hong Kong. At my church rummage sale, I purchased a set of six shallow pottery bowls: cobalt blue on the inside and unglazed on the outside. The deep blue glasses were found at a garage sale on a Sunday after leaving church. Ray uses the light blue, deep ceramic bowl each morning, heaping it to the rim with yogurt and frozen blueberries and raspberries.

Ray prepares for Advent outdoors by hanging blue lights around the entrance of the grotto. This special place deserves its own story.

For seven years after purchasing acreage until our move from Chicago, we spent our summer vacations here at Bakken [in the foothills of the Cascade Mountains in northwestern Washington.] The first summer we had only a tent and an outhouse. By the next summer we had a 20x14 one-room cabin made of logs salvaged from a prior owner's beginning attempt to build a log house.

One summer Ray tackled the job of clearing garbage out of a secluded pocket of tall cedars. The trash thrown there included surprisingly large discards: a pink bathtub, several washbasins, and a car door. Ray took two full pickup loads to the county dump. When all was cleared out, he invited me to come and see the transformed space, saying now we had an outdoor room. What should we do with it?

I pronounced it a grotto and asked him to make benches and a table. We ate many noon meals there on hot days during those vacations. Once we began identifying places at Bakken, it acquired a name: Mary of Nazareth Grotto. Ray

11

handpainted a sign for it. He then wanted an image of Mary, a Mary who looked Semitic.

Sam Gore, a sculptor and friend of our family, had wanted an excuse to enlarge his small figure of Mary carrying her child. Sam invited Hannah, a young teenager from Lebanon, to model as he reshaped the face with Semitic features. That bronze casting now stands in the grotto. Sam came to supervise the installation. In that secluded place, lighting was needed. Sam wanted a mixture of warm and cool colors: red and blue, one from either side. The historic Church has given significance to those colors: red for theology and blue for humanity. In Orthodox iconography, as Mother of God, Mary wears both colors.

We have hosted Advent meditations in the grotto, bundled in blankets, drinking hot cider.

One year we hosted an Advent party. Carol, Ray's assistant, asked whether I would host the annual Christmas party for Bakke Graduate University staff. They wanted to drive the ninety miles from Seattle to Bakken and had selected the evening of Sunday, December 3.

I had attended the previous staff Christmas parties in homes beautifully decorated for Christmas. On December 3, my house would be decorated for Advent. I asked: Could it be an Advent party? They graciously agreed. None of us had ever been to an Advent party, but all were willing to enter into the adventure. I asked that everyone dress in an Advent color: purple, pink, or blue, but not red or green.

Previous parties included gift exchanges. I asked that each person bring a small, gift-wrapped (in Advent colors) box to place on the dinner table as a decoration. The box need not contain a gift, only a hint of a gift to be given at Christmas. Each person would choose one of the gift-wrapped boxes, open [it], and try to guess the intended gift.

A lavish number of votive candles, placed on windowsills, welcomed the guests. We began with music: "Sleigh Ride" by Leroy Anderson, arranged for duet and expanded for the occasion to include sleigh bells, Chinese wood block, and coronet. With angklungs (bamboo instruments from Indonesia played by shaking) handed to everyone, we played "Joy to the World" and "Edelweiss."

12

I sewed matching aprons of dark blue for Carol and me to wear as we became waitresses and served dinner restaurant style. After we cleared away dirty dishes, the decorative boxes were opened, one by one. Stories were told around the table, explaining the planning and excitement involved in each gift to be given.

Carol's box contained a single chess piece. She explained about her husband's love of the game. He taught one of their four sons to play chess at age five. That little boy grew up, married and had a son whom he taught to play chess by that same age. The single chess piece symbolized an antique chess set found among her father-in-law's possessions, a surprising discovery since the family had no memory of him playing chess. Carol was excitedly looking forward to wrapping the chess set for her son as a Christmas gift from Grandpa.

Advent activities at Bakken are incomplete without a visit to the grotto. Everyone dressed for outside and walked down the steep path lined with lights. After returning to the warmth of the house, we ate dessert by candlelight and concluded with the reading of a story.

It is the season of expectation. We wait.

Corean and her husband Ray live at Bakken where she divides her time between music, writing, designing worship, hosting, and maintaining her home and gardens. She may be contacted at corean.bakke@gmail.com for information about ordering her books.

JESUS CHRIST, WE SING TO YOU

Jesus Christ, we sing to you,
born to visit earth and die;
Jesus Christ, we give you praise,
risen and returning soon.

Expectations we hold close
in this place of joy and loss.

Guide your Church and keep her safe.
Give her mission in your name.

When disaster rends our world,
filling us with fear and dread,
in the darkness shine your light.
Transform chaos into peace.

As you came in Bethlehem,
come to us in Word and wine.
As you call us to respond,
faithfully we follow you.

Refrain:

God with us, Immanuel.
We your people watch and wait.

This essay and song, composed by Corean Bakke, have been used by her permission, excerpted from her excellent guide for living the seasons of the church year, Practicing the Church Year: A Spirituality for the Home. *"Jesus Christ, We Sing to You" and her other hymns may be found in her book,* Aleluya: Singing the Church Year.

MONDAY. Expecting Something That Matters. *Sarah Styles Bessey*

I've already set out my plain, white pillar candles in anticipation of this coming Sunday, the start of Advent. They're perched in a sea of river stones, on a black slate plate, on my kitchen table. We lay our treasures from our daily walks onto these stones; small pine cones, bright red leaves, a sprig from the hemlock. Flotsam and jetsam are resting between the unlit wicks, waiting for Jesus to breathe life reborn again. It's my made-up Advent wreath, a cobbling together of my version of the Church tradition and I think it says something about me, but I'm not sure what.

He's coming soon; so what do I expect?

He's coming soon, the Christ child. This year, I am eager for the liturgy, eager for the prayers of the saints spoken by so many lips for so many years, for the lighting of the candles. **A happy-clappy antiestablishment Jesus follower, am I, and yet these rituals have become one of the most important parts of my year.** The liturgy and holiness, tracing the line of time backwards through saints and sisters, matters to me. It pulls me away from commercialization, from crass misrepresentation. The practice of Advent gives me an exhale, a focus, an active waiting.

There is also the mother-part of me that always lines up with Mary, Mother of God, to wait with her in anticipation. (If there is one thing that mothers come to understand as they grow heavy with life, as they mother small souls in all their storming and resting and growing and learning, it's *waiting*.)

And then there is me in the world—waiting, aching, yearning, for the restoration of all things, for the beautiful redemption of all pain, all sorrow, all brokenness. Advent is just as much about waiting for what God has yet to do as it is the commemoration of what he has already done. And those lines, *the now and not yet*, they blur for me most days, a tension.

So do I expect my version of the Messiah? Do I expect a soon-coming King to overthrow an evil empire and set all things to right as I see fit? (Apparently, I am no different than a group of Galileans and Zealots two thousand years ago.) My eye is already kingdom-focused, the work of the Church one of making space for God's way of life and true humanity. Or do I expect Jesus, the Christ?

A kingdom that moves not by armies and decrees and laws written in stone, but one that moves like yeast, like a seed, written in the hearts and flesh of people like us?

My expectation this year, in my honest self, knee-deep in living, is only this: **Make it matter to me**.

Jesus, make the fact that you came, the fact that you are still arriving, *matter* in my life. **My life should show the new dawn**, my heart, my brain, my soul, the very lines on my face should show how the glory of God is the woman fully alive, truly human. I read a phrase of Eugene Peterson's once and he called this God-life one of "robust sanity."

So I've got my candles set up. My Bible is open, my Book of Common Prayer beside. My other faithful, oft-underlined companion of Advent, *Accompanied by Angels: Poems of the Incarnation*, by Luci Shaw, waits.

I pray my soul will welcome always that small
seed. That I will hail it when it enters me.

I don't mind being grit, soil, dirt, mud-brown,
laced with the rot of old leaves, if only the seed

can find me, find a home and bear a fruit,
sweet, flushed, full-fleshed – a glory apple.[7]

On my lips, one prayer for these Advent weeks, wherever it may lead: **Be it unto me, as You have said.** I'm waiting, watching, a midwife of the Kingdom.

Sarah Bessey is the author of Jesus Feminist, *a disarming and beautiful invitation to the Kingdom of God waiting on the other side of the Church's gender debates. She is an award-winning blogger at* www.sarahbessey.com, *an editor at* A Deeper Story, *a contributor for* SheLoves Magazine, *and a passionate advocate for global women's justice issues. She lives in Abbotsford, British Columbia, Canada, with her husband and their three tinies.*

---

[7] Luci Shaw. "I gave this Day to God." *Accompanied by Angels: Poems of the Incarnation* (Grand Rapids: William B. Eerdmans Publishing Company, 2006), 25.

TUESDAY. Mary and Mindfulness, *Kristin Carroccino*

I am trying to teach my children mindfulness. In my tireless effort to teach them to "mind" me, this would seem an exercise in futility. Yet this powerful and simple connection of noticing one's breath—one's life force, Spirit indwelling, is the lesson I most want them to learn. To listen deeply to themselves and the great love within. To God within. Incarnation. To come home to themselves. And, like any good teacher learns with much practice and difficulty, one must be on the same learning path as the student; in this case, my wildly creative and precocious children.

So, we simply ring a meditation bell. A primitive wooden mallet strikes the small brass bowl, and the bell hums. We are learning to stop when we hear the bell and breathe deep, re-membering our thoughts and intentions. This is the essence of this Advent I desire most. Moments will build upon moments. Three breaths will become ten and, eventually, a different lens with which to experience the "monkey mind" of the world that surrounds us.

I, like Mary, was great with child one Advent season. My son was delivered about a month and several thousand years after hers, and during those first years of small babies, then sweet and bumbling toddlers, I learned to know a very different Mary than the woman I encountered in my youth. This Mary, like me, ambled slowly in the late months of the year, and when her son arrived, felt overwhelmed about what to do with this new little human (and, let's be honest, probably a lot more overwhelmed than me given the circumstances of his conception…). As her son grew and other siblings joined the brood, she, like me, became overwhelmed with the chaos in the hut and asked the older children to go outside and play, or to go see if Joseph needed any help over in the workshop.

And then, one blustery day, Mary must have discovered her own meditation bell, some way of helping the noise of the house cease upon a word or sound and slow for a few moments. She invited everyone to "come home" and feel the light radiating within. I know this must have happened, because the son that grew up to become a Rabbi was a master at producing calm in a crowd. He could quiet stormy seas, demons, the multitudes. One can't preach what one

17

doesn't practice. We know from the Bible that Jesus sometimes went away, alone, to pray. The most famous prolonged recorded experience of this is just before Jesus began his public ministry, when he went into the desert to face himself.

If you've ever gone on a retreat, alone, for a few days, or even spent a few hours alone during the time of life when you may be surrounded by many children and their various activities, you may have experienced something similar to me: at first relief, brief contentment, then a sort of dull panic. What do I do with this time? How do I spend this time with myself? Who am I really? Who, or What is God? It doesn't take long to get to those essential and hugely intimidating questions of life, the ones for which adventurers and seekers are often said to be climbing mountains to find gurus to provide answers.

Jesus was one of the bravest and most radical souls all those millennia ago. He walked out into the desert, into the stark quiet to face himself. He couldn't have done that without growing up in Mary's household. All those years spent as an infant, then child, then teenager in her Nazareth cottage led to that moment when he walked out into the wilderness alone and came back ready and on fire to love fiercely and change the world. Mary's prayers, Mary's meditation bells, Mary's understanding that you have to "come home" to yourself before you can provide freedom for others.

So this Advent season, we will wait with anticipation the two comings of Christ and we will practice, in our own small and simple ways, that same coming moment by moment in each day as we come home to ourselves—when we remember to breathe—and stop—when we hear the full, round hum of our bell. And thus, we will change the world.

Kristin is a writer, editor, and visual artist who lives in Seattle with her husband, two children, and an energetic small dog. She volunteers as a writer/editor for Mustard Seed Associates and tries to spend as much time in nature as possible.

WEDNESDAY. Waiting With Ants.
Jim Fisher

A boy, not much older than a toddler, is sitting cross-legged on the sidewalk in front of his house, staring at a crack in the cement. As I approach him from the end of the block, I slow my pace so as not to interrupt whatever has captivated his attention.

With a light smile on my face, I stand amazed at the intensity of his focus. His head, resting on his hands, has not moved for several minutes. Then as he turns to pick up a small stick, he catches sight of me watching him. Without showing any signs of being startled, he simply greets me with a cheerful, "Hi!"

"Hi, Jimmy. What are you studying so intently?"

"Ants," he replies excitedly.

"What are the ants doing?"

Jimmy turns, points his little stick to the crack in the sidewalk and explains, "Well, they go down into the ground through this hole and bring up sand. Then they carry it up over this pile and drop it and then go back down into the ground to get some more."

As I sit on the pavement next to him, I watch as ants excavate their underground tunnels and build the perfectly round dome of sand that we all have seen in the cracks of sidewalks. As an adult, I certainly would never take the time, even on a perfect day like this, to sit and study … and wait … with the intensity and awe of this little boy. I begin to wonder why.

Jimmy returns to his study and lightly disturbs the dome with his stick to explore how the ants scurry to mend the scar. Amazed at his inquisitive spirit, I ask, "Do you study ants often?"

"Just when Mommy is gone."

Startled, I probe deeper, "You mean your mom is not in the house?"

"No. She went shopping. She told me to wait here until she got back." Jimmy's forehead wrinkles. He is starting to wonder why I am asking these questions.

I hesitantly ask one more, "How long has she been gone?"

19

"Since after breakfast, I guess."

It was almost noon.

Immersed in my adult worldview, I am having a hard time with this. I live in a time of child abductions, child abandonment, and abuse. I live in a time of constant stimulus, handheld phones, electronic games, and social media. I live in a time of attention deficit and instant gratification. I live in a time where no responsible parent would leave their three-year-old child outside to wait for her return hours later.

I also live in a time when we have lost our desire, and maybe even our ability, to wait.

I am finding this especially difficult because I am peering back more than half a century to a very different time. I am also peering back to a very different person ... for that little boy is me.

I have lost that childlike sense of awe and wonder-filled anticipation of what comes next. Well maybe not lost, but certainly scribbled over with ink drawn from the well of societal pressures, expectations, and norms. I tend to wait with twiddling thumbs, not with the active, anticipatory patience of a child.

The little boy knows that his mother will return. He has no reason to question it. And as he catches sight of her pulling the wagon full of groceries at the end of the block, he jumps on his tricycle pedaling as fast as his little legs will allow, scurrying to greet her. And as they return to the house, once again united and engaged with each other, I wonder. I wonder if I will have that same childlike enthusiasm and energy to greet Jesus when He returns to us here on Earth. I wonder if I really understand what the [end of the world] is going to be like. I wonder if I really understand Advent.

I wonder, too, how ants with brains smaller than the grains of sand they are carrying can have such a perfected sense of symmetry and order. How can they instinctively know how to work together for the common good when we humans with much larger brains have yet to figure that out? Will I and the rest of humanity, our Creator's crown jewel, ever learn how to care for and love our planet and each other as we were intended? How shall I wait for that? Like an adult waiting for a bus? Or like a child.

Lord, teach me to wait with the heart and energy of that little boy within me. Lead me away from a purposeless passing of the time and toward purpose-filled anticipation. Guide me in Your purposes and keep me moving on a path, mending the scars on our planet and our people so that we become worthy of Your return. Amen.

Jim Fisher enjoys reading and listening to stories. On his best days, he paints word-pictures for his website, which you can find by searching for "Holy Hugs" via Google. He lives in Minnesota with his wife, Mary, his bicycle, Renée, and his 15-year-old narcissistic moth orchid, Luna, who always starts to bloom during Advent and continues her showy display until Easter.

THURSDAY. Remember Our Story,
Ellen Haroutunian

Our world is unraveling. We are seeing the deterioration of civil society in many ways. The Thanksgiving holiday week alone has been an embarrassment of aggressive consumerism with shoppers resorting to pepper spray and robbing each other at gunpoint. Black Friday is extending back into Thursday, threatening to diminish the one day we have set aside to pause our frantic lives and give thanks that some of us actually have money to spend. And that's just the news on the small scale.

I just had a long conversation with a friend over the meaning of Christmas. It began around her assertion that Christmas has nothing to do with Jesus. When you look at Wal-Mart at midnight on Thanksgiving, you can see that that has become very true. But the conversation was more about how many choose to celebrate Christmas either in a secular fashion or with more ancient ties to the pagan rituals that were the inspiration for the choice of December for this observance. I agreed, the holiday was birthed from engagement with other traditions and has taken on many more dimensions, much of which have nothing to do with the remembering of Jesus and the Christian story. I also agreed with her that people should be allowed to celebrate how they wish without harassment. In her insistence that Christmas has nothing to do with Jesus, I assume she wanted to show support for the millions who celebrate Christmas in various ways, but have no Christian affiliation.

Even so, it's important to remember that the shaping of the Christmas celebration (long before secular commercialization) was intentional and beautiful. Early Christians brought their story to the celebrations that they had already been observing, such as pagan solstice rituals, or more likely, the Roman solar celebration. Since the beginning of time, people had observed that light returns to the world as the world revolves around the sun, renewing and enlivening as it comes. The Christian story, the gospel story, is about the Light coming into the world, bringing life and healing to hurting souls. What was already observed and celebrated in rhythm with creation was then seen to hold a deeper meaning in the minds of these early Christians. As a result, the season of waiting (Advent) and the celebration of the Incarnation of God, Emmanuel, was born. Eventually, the season became known as the Feast of the Nativity or Christ's Mass. So, on the level of tradition and history, the evolution of Christmas as a holiday (holy day) is indeed about Jesus. The whole point of the discussion was that there's no need to diminish Christian tradition to make room for other traditions, just as there's no need to diminish other traditions to make space for the Christian.

But that discussion isn't the true issue. I understand that there is a lot of anger towards Christians who have been offering judgment instead of the Good News. I understand that people would then choose to diminish the Christian Story as a result. That's what people do. That's why the world is hurting. We all diminish and deny the traditions, beliefs, needs and feelings of *the other* in order to make space for ourselves. However, in doing so, any empathy for *the other* is also lost. Lack of empathy for *the other* is the human heart in its most desolate state. The particular case above was about diminishing Christianity. But the way of thinking that essentially diminishes or eliminates *the other,* any *other,* has become the norm worldwide as each of our hearts shrink and pull back into self-protective bunkers. This is what our broken and hard-hearted system of justice does.

So, we live in a world in which empathy is a rare gem. More than ever, this has become a world of every man or woman for themselves, whether it be about grabbing the last waffle maker at Wal-Mart, or blocking job-creating bills because you don't like the politics of the party in power, or insisting that every conservative Christian is hate-filled and every liberal one is immoral, or that every Muslim is a terrorist. We no longer seek to listen, to know, to honor and respect each other. We no longer see the Image in one another. The idea of being our brothers' keeper has become laughable, even amongst Jesus followers. We cannot compromise and work together because whatever *the other* represents is simply too offensive, too threatening, too inconvenient, too irrelevant to our personal lives. In this sense, we indeed have truly lost Jesus.

We do not need to create a "let's take Christmas back" mentality. That is not what this essay is about, and it's only another way to diminish those with whom we disagree. We do acknowledge that millions of people who are not Christians celebrate "Christmas" in various ways around the world and can remain unthreatened by that. However, the most important thing we can do is to reflect to the world the Light that has come to us. The incarnation of God-as-human is an act of ultimate empathy. God, who is Wholly Other became *the other* in order to love fully and to reconcile, to heal, to save. This is what love does! Love enters the story of *the other.* This world that has become more cold and hard and cynical than ever is desperate for a love that enters in.

23

Remember the Story. May we remember and act accordingly and thus bring true empathy back into the world, whether it's at Wal-Mart or in Congress or towards Wall Street protestors or in trying to be politically correct (or not). The world says, "Your needs and pain don't matter to me" as it steps on the heads of the weaker brother to move upward towards bigger and better. Jesus calls us back down to our senses, back down to being our brothers' and sisters' keepers, back down to a life of love. And when we listen to his Story, we find that he has shown us how.

The true light that enlightens every man was coming into the world. (John 1:9 Revised Standard Version)

Definitions of Empathy:

1. The imaginative projection of a subjective state into an object, so that the object appears to be infused with it *(perhaps incarnates it?—my addition).*

2. The action of understanding, being aware of, being sensitive to, and vicariously experiencing the feelings, thoughts, and experience of another of either the past or present without having the feelings, thoughts, and experience fully communicated in an objectively explicit manner; *also* : the capacity for this.

Ellen Haroutunian is a therapist, spiritual director, writer and urban pastor. She lives in Lakewood, Colorado, with her husband and two retired racing greyhounds.

FRIDAY. Let Us Wait as Children Wait.
Coe Hutchison

Let us wait as children wait—for the Child. How do children wait?

On pins and needles. In anticipation. There is no question of whether what is being anticipated will arrive, there is only a question of when. It is hard to sit still, the excitement is so great. Let's wiggle, let's fidget. Is it time? Is it time?

We are excited, we anticipate because we know it will be good. How do we know it will be good? Because we have heard the stories, we know the stories by heart. The stories of His coming, the stories of His gifts, the stories of His love. We know it will be good. There is no question, no doubt, it will be *very* good.

As we wait we strain to hear. Do I hear Him there? Is that Him speaking? Is that His voice I hear in another person? Is that His voice I hear in a hymn or song? Is that His voice I hear in the hustle and bustle of the season? Is that His voice in the bank teller, or the exhausted retail worker? Is that His voice in my coworker or the grocery checker? Is that His voice in my family? Is He speaking through those at the Food Bank, at the Shelter? We listen for His voice wherever we are, whatever we are doing. We strain to hear Him.

As we wait we strain to see. Is that Him there? Is that Him in the video, the movie? Is that Him in the church pew next to me? Is that Him in the children's Christmas pageant? Is He there in the nursing home resident, the hospital patient? Is He there in our worship, in our shopping, in our celebrating? Is that Him there in our family? We strain to see Him.

As we stretch our ears to hear, as we strain our eyes to see, we are attuned to His voice, and our eyes are trained to spot His face. And we do hear Him. We do see Him. Let us watch and listen as children watch and listen, for we *will* see and hear Him. We know the stories, we know the promises, it will be good, it will be *very* good. Let us wait, and watch, and anticipate, and fidget, as children do. "For unto us a child is born and his name shall be called Wonderful, Counsellor, The mighty God, The everlasting Father, Prince of Peace." I can't wait. I can't wait!

Coe Hutchison is pastor of Grace Lutheran Church in Port Townsend, Washington, former Board chair and good friend of Mustard Seed Associates.

BLACK FRIDAY. Consumption vs. Community. *Katie Metzger*

Black Friday[8] shopping has become an American holiday tradition on par with pumpkin pie, Christmas trees, and roasting a turkey. The popularity of this post-Thanksgiving pastime has increased exponentially over the last decade with many stores opening their doors on Thanksgiving evening and several people, each year, dying in the midst of this craziness. How does this display of overconsumption relate to a holiday that is supposed to be centered on giving thanks? How does our need to consume affect those around us? These questions are not only pertinent to how our choices affect local workers and the environment, but those around the globe who manufacture our goods as well.

The mainstream clothing industry has historically been credited with gross underpayment of its workers and inhumane working conditions. On average, 80 percent of the clothing we buy in the western world is made utilizing unethical means. Sweatshops from Bangladesh to Cambodia routinely pay their workers around $1.20 per day for their work. This is not a living wage, even in poverty-stricken communities. The chronic underpayment of garment industry workers creates a cycle of poverty in already struggling communities, in turn contributing to other community social issues resulting from poverty.

Sweatshops are not only present in developing nations, but are also a growing problem in the United States. Many people assume that if an item of clothing sports the "Made in the USA" logo, it is not produced in a sweatshop, however that is often not the case. According to the U.S. Department of Labor, as recently as the year 2000, 11,000 U.S. based factories were cited as violating workers' rights and not paying laborers a minimum wage.[9] This shows that the problem of human rights violations in textile and garment factories is not only an international problem, but a domestic problem as well.

If inhumane treatment of workers is often the norm in the clothing industry, how can we support a new system that embraces the spirit of thanks and

---

[8] Editor's Note: "Black Friday" is the day after Thanksgiving in the United States and refers to the idea that, traditionally, retailers operated "in the red" from January to November. "Black Friday" is the supposed day that stores begin to turn a profit and is said to be the busiest shopping day of the year. "Cyber Monday," in the following week is a more recent phenomenon and refers to Internet shopping.

[9] "Economic Action to End Sweatshop and Forced Child Labor"
http://www.greenamerica.org/programs/sweatshops/whattoknow.cfm

community? Making a conscious decision to buy locally and to seek out fair trade goods can have a huge impact on the clothing industry as a whole. A 2011 Harvard study found that consumers are willing to pay 5-10% more for items they know are ethically made and that adding a third-party designated fair-trade label increases sales by 10% on average.[10] Although large strides towards ethical production have been made in the coffee, chocolate, and food industry, the clothing industry remains hugely underserved. Some options for supporting a more just clothing system are:

1. Realize that someone is paying the price for your clothing…is it you or the garment worker? Jeans should cost more than $9.99. When you encounter clothing that is extremely cheap ask yourself, "what kind of production practices lend to producing a $3 tank top?" The answer is usually pretty obvious.

2. Inform yourself about your favorite brands. It is well-known that companies such as Forever 21, H&M, Victoria's Secret, and Wal-Mart have unethical supply chains. However, information is severely lacking for many brands. Do some digging online and if nothing is available, request information.

3. If you are unsure, shop local and secondhand. Finding local markets and boutiques supports your local economy and makes it easier to engage in conversation and get information. Also, secondhand and vintage shopping can be a cost-effective and fun way to go!

4. Start exploring and support fair trade fashion companies. Finding fair trade clothing that is actually fashionable can be a struggle. Many fair trade clothing companies are either insanely expensive or produce clothing you wouldn't want to wear. However, lately there has been a surge of new fashionable clothing companies that are competitively priced. Support these new change-makers in revolutionizing the clothing industry.

Next time you are shopping for clothing, whether it is Black Friday or any other time of the year, I urge you to consider the implications of your choices. Where you choose to spend your money and assert your purchasing power perpetuates a system of ideals. Let thanks, love, and a sense of community dictate what your dollar supports.

---

[10] Hainmueller, Jens and Hiscox, Michael J. and Sequeira, Sandra, "Consumer Demand for the Fair Trade Label: Evidence from a Multi-Store Field Experiment" (March 2014). Review of Economics and Statistics, Forthcoming; Formerly: MIT Political Science Department Research Paper No. 2011-9B

Katie is a Pacific Northwest native and cofounder of Same Thread Apparel, a fashion-forward social enterprise that helps to empower women in northern Thailand by creating financial sustainability. She completed her master's degree in International Community Development from Northwest University where she initially developed an interest in social justice and social enterprise. In addition to her work with Same Thread Apparel, Katie works with Mustard Seed Associates as their administrator. She lives and works in Seattle, with her husband and two dogs. For more information about Same Thread Apparel, visit www.samethread.com.

SATURDAY. *Gather, Feast, Create*

Gather

In the United States, Thanksgiving is celebrated on the Thursday of this week, shoppers rose before dawn to take advantage of deep discounts at shopping malls on Black Friday, and lots of folks are traveling to or recovering from the holiday feast. On this Saturday, try something new and slow things down and gather with a small group of friends, neighbors, people from your community

of worship, or your immediate family and enjoy a simple, relaxed meal. As you dine, discuss various ways to approach the upcoming weeks, such as alternative gift-giving, celebrating the "feast" days of the saints of the season, and setting this time aside each week to rejoin and refocus on the Advent to Lent journey.

At the end of the feast, create a resource for counting the days of Advent for each person or family to enjoy at home. You might also enjoy praying Christine's prayer and singing the verse of "O Come, O Come Emmanuel" that corresponds to the O Adonai antiphon: "O come, O come, Thou Lord of might/who to The tribes on Sinai's height/in ancient times did give the law/in cloud and majesty and awe. Rejoice! Rejoice! Emmanuel Shall Come to Thee, O Israel!"

Feast

Meal: Simple soup, salad, and bread potluck

Keep this week's meal simple and prepare one or two simple soups and salads, and some hearty bread if you love to bake (if you don't, seek out a local baker in your community and reheat a handmade loaf in the oven and serve with plenty of butter).

Create

In this week of preparing, there are limitless ideas of how to physically mark the passing of days from Advent to Christmas. The free Resources download at msaimagine.com as well as Internet searches offer myriad forms of Advent wreaths, calendars, Jesse trees, Advent jars, chains, and many other beautiful and delightful formats to help us count the days. Choose one or two and create and craft together as you swap stories of past Christmas seasons and plan for this one.

—Kristin

O REX GENTIUM

"O sacred Lord of ancient Israel, the only joy of every human heart; O keystone of the mighty arch of man, come and save the creature you fashioned from the dust."

Week One of Advent

[Image: Mansion of Baron A.L. Steiglitz]

O King of
Nations

Advent means coming, and the season beckons us towards three comings that should inspire and renew us as we move towards Christmas day.

The first is the remembrance of Jesus coming in the flesh, an infant whose birth captivates our hearts yet makes few, if any demands on our souls. For many, the story is nothing more than a children's story, a soothing tale that is little more than an add-on to the secular celebration of consumption and overindulgence.

The next coming to which Advent calls our attention is the coming of the presence of God recognized among us now in the Scripture, in the Eucharist, in the community itself. This coming makes Jesus present in our own lives, eternally enlivening, eternally with us.

The final coming to which Advent points us is what my husband Tom calls Advent II homecoming, the return of Christ at the end of time. It is the hope of this coming that whets our souls with a deep longing for the wholeness, peace and abundance of God's emerging eternal world for which we should strive with every breath.

This, Frederick Buechner tells us, is where we belong. It is home, and whether we realize it or not, I think we are all of us homesick for it.

In her book *The Liturgical Year*, Joan Chittister writes, "The function of Advent is to remind us what we're waiting for as we go through life too busy with things that do not matter to remember the things that do." [11] She goes on to challenge us: "Advent asks the question, what is it for which you are spending your life?"[12]

We all desperately crave more-meaningful, less-cluttered lives. More than that, we all long for the home that God has prepared for us, the home towards which the season of Advent beckons us. Yet we rarely take the time to slow down and give up the urgent for the important. In preparation for Christmas this year, consider Joan Chittister's challenge. What is it for which you are spending your life?

—Christine

---

[11] Joan Chittister, *The Liturgical Year* (Nashville: Thomas Nelson, 2009), 61.
[12] Chittister, 62.

Prayer for Week One of Advent

Lord Jesus Christ we await your coming.
We wait filled with hope,
knowing your light will shine in the darkness.
We wait anticipating your peace,
believing that one day it will fill our world.
We wait embracing your love.
May we reach out to share it with our neighbours.
We wait with joy,
bubbling up in expectation of your birth.
Lord we wait.
Come soon and fill us with your life.

—Christine

Edward Hicks, "Peaceable Kingdom" Public Domain

SUNDAY. Sin, Redemption, and the
Path of Healing. *Becca Stevens*

The theological notions of sin and redemption contain a heaviness that stems from the fact that they are mostly used to point out the faults in others, rather than to free us from the traps that prevent us from loving God. In the ninth chapter of the Gospel of John, when Jesus leaves the synagogue after arguing about right beliefs and old customs, he encounters a blind man who is begging. In this narrative Jesus preaches a radical way to approach sin and redemption in our life of faith. It's an approach that offers a deeper way of understanding the terms. Instead of being heavy, it lifts our hearts and minds with the lightness of grace. When the disciples of Jesus see the blind man, they ask, "Who sinned, this man or his parents…?" The implication in the question is that if the blind man is a sinner, we don't have to respond, because the man's blindness itself is a sign of divine punishment for sin. The only pertinent question for them is "Who is to blame?"

Characteristically, Jesus uses the question as an opportunity to teach them that culpability—establishing guilt or responsibility for sin—is the not the issue we need to address in the suffering we encounter in our world. Jesus through his action and words reminds us all that the issue of morality and culpability lies in our response to suffering and in our ability to love with compassion, not judgment. Then Jesus, with nothing but spit and dirt, makes a healing and soothing mud for the man. This beautiful, simple, earthy action reminds us that redemption is always possible, even when we feel incapable to adequately address the sin and suffering we meet along the way. The whole story breathes life into the old theologies of blame and exclusion written in stone. It gives us a path to walk where sin and redemption become matters of freeing ourselves, not condemning others. For the blind man, like all of us, sin and redemption were terms others used that alienated and condemned him. For Jesus, sin and redemption become the absolution that frees us to live in gratitude for a loving and merciful God.

Last week, National Public Radio aired four separate features on the women who live in the residential community of Magdalene and its social enterprise, Thistle Farms. The women of Magdalene, who have survived lives of addiction and prostitution, are offered sanctuary for two years to find the path of freedom for themselves. Maybe no other group in our culture has been more maligned and assigned the term "sinner." One of the women featured on the series was

Penny Hall, a forty-eight-year-old woman who has been clean and off the streets for four years. Penny was raised in a beer hall in Nashville, Tennessee, and spent six years under a bridge prostituting and using crack. Today she runs the manufacturing department at Thistle Farms that produces healing oils and thistle paper. After harvesting thistles, turning them into beautiful paper, then folding that paper into boxes, Penny fills them with bottles that hold a mixture of oils, really balms. She sends these lovely boxes around the country for people to use in healing—for themselves and others. To see her today is to witness the very incarnation of redemption and hope.

Penny describes her own transformation with "I used to have black eyes, now I have cucumber eyes." It took me a long time to understand what she meant, until finally one day I understood that she meant it literally. She used to have black eyes—eyes that were bruised and beaten. Her prayer was that when she slept, she wouldn't be raped or robbed. She lived in fear and isolation, with the reality that thrives in sick communities that feed on each other. She lived in communities that rationalize that it's her fault, so it's not our issue. The truth is, though, that Penny didn't get to the streets by herself; it took all kinds of people and a broken community to get her there. And so it takes a community to help her come home.

Penny describes her eyes now as "cucumber." She feels like she has felt the richness of the fruit placed on the eyes to heal and soothe them. Those are eyes that are comforted and consoled, that are seen as worthy. It is a powerful analogy for sin and redemption, signaling the healing nature that lies on the path between the two. On our journey, the one we all take, when we are graced with feeling the movement from sin to redemption, we can feel our own eyes move from black to cucumber. When we see how we have crossed that path with all the grace and mud and cucumbers people have given us along the way, we can use the words sin and redemption for our own lives, feel the freedom they offer, and then live in gratitude, hoping for the chance to love others the way we have been loved, lavishly, without judgment, without guilt or blame. Jesus calls us to love the whole world, one person at a time. Love in the Gospel is always preached in action and along the spiritual path of sin and redemption. It is what we are given. It is what we give. We are called to offer our best, whether it is cucumbers or mud, for the sake of soothing and healing.

This piece is used by permission from Becca Steven's blog *beccastevens.org*. It was originally published there on May 5, 2011.

Becca Stevens is a preacher, speaker, Episcopal priest, and founder of Magdalene, residential communities of women who have survived prostitution, trafficking and addiction. She founded Thistle Farms in 2001, which currently employs nearly 50 residents and graduates, and houses a natural body care line, a paper and sewing studio and the Thistle Stop Café. Becca is the author of Snake Oil: The Art of Healing and Truth-Telling *and the forthcoming* The Way of Tea and Justice: Rescuing the World's Favorite Beverage from its Violent History. *She lives in Nashville, Tennessee, with her family.*

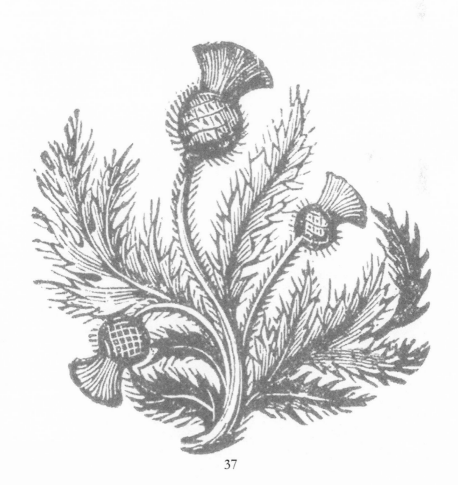

MONDAY. What is the Future You Want to Come Home to? *Tom Sine*

During the season of Advent, I suspect most of us can call up some of our very best memories of coming home to a place of festivity and welcome by those who love us. Unfortunately that is not true for everyone.

I just came back from the bank on a beautiful, brisk sunny day. For the first time, I sensed that the teller, I will call Tamara, was troubled. She told me today that she is from Syria. Tamara, with evident concern, admitted that she is not sure if her parents are safe or not. I left the bank with a sinking feeling that she has no idea if she will ever come home again or if her parents will survive the ongoing violence.

As we celebrated Advent in 2013, there were over 2 million Syrians who were not only refugees, also at risk because of the ongoing war. At least 600,000 Filipinos were homeless, and countries all over the world were rushing to their aid. There were at least 172,000 Haitians in temporary shelters after the earthquake that destroyed their homes in 2010. Finally, there were still around 1.5 million Palestinians living in 58 refugee camps created decades ago on the West Bank, Gaza, Jordon, Lebanon and other countries in the region that had little hope of coming home.

As followers of Jesus, how we respond to the urgent needs of our many homeless neighbors will be determined in part by notions of the future we believe Jesus invites us to come home to.

I was not raised in the church. I was converted into an evangelical faith. I was taught that coming home to God's eternal world was all about my disembodied spirit going up to a nonmaterial world in the clouds. Many people nurtured in this faith are still singing a song that I believe has more to do with the writings of Plato than the teachings of Jesus...."This world is not my home...I am just a passing through."

Doesn't popular eschatological literature of escape invite us to imagine going up at the rapture...leaving our clothes behind on airplane seats and leaving all the suffering behind? My first concern with this view of God's purposes for the human future is that I am convinced it isn't biblical. My second concern is that people who hold this view often seem to have very little concern for those that are left behind or even for the urgent needs that fill our world today.

Don't most of the songs that Christians sing about coming home seem to be about us going up instead of Jesus coming down? We urgently need song writers to help us find some new images about coming home to this good world being restored and not destroyed.

In *Surprised by Hope*, N.T. Wright invites us to rediscover a biblical vision of coming home that is not to a disembodied existence in the clouds. Instead, he reminds us that the scripture teaches that that Jesus is coming down, the New Jerusalem is coming down…we are not going up. He argues convincingly from 1 Corinthians 15 that we will come home to a restored creation as a great bodily resurrected intercultural community…real bodies, but different bodies just like our risen Leader.

One cannot read the Gospels or the prophets without realizing that God's loving purposes are not just about changing us spiritually…as important as that is. God in Christ intends to make all things new. I am looking forward to coming home to a future in which the blind see, the deaf hear and lame run. I am looking forward to coming home to a future in which the broken are healed and all the refugees find their way home. I look forward to a future in which justice finally comes for the poor and oppressed, and peace comes to the nations. I look forward to coming home to a future in which God's good creation isn't destroyed, but restored with great celebration.

So Advent for me is always a great celebration of our best memories of coming home. But it is also an anticipatory celebration of the return of Christ, when all things are finally made new.

Can I suggest this is not only a season of anticipation and celebration, but a season of calling? Aren't we called during this season of Advent to follow Jesus by making God's purposes our purposes? Aren't we called not to seek life but to lose life in service to God and others? Shouldn't we as followers of Jesus recommit our lives to God's loving purposes for a people and a world?

I come to this season looking forward to Christine and I cooking and celebrating with friends old and new. It is my favorite season of the year. I am already planning the meals I want to prepare.

But this year, I feel nudged to find an intentional way to be a bit of God's good news in my community every week. I made a telephone call before I wrote this essay to find a place where I can make a little difference, locally.

How is God inviting you during this season of Advent to not only celebrate the great homecoming, but also to give expression to it in your neighborhood or God's larger world?

Tom Sine is research guy at Mustard Seed Associates and hospitality guy at the Mustard Seed House. He has worked for many years as a consultant in futures research and planning for both Christian and secular organizations. His latest book is The New Conspirators. *Tom blogs weekly at* msaimagine.org.

TUESDAY. Simple Faith.
Paula Mitchell

Jesus, life of the world, Word of the Father, the one who holds all things together, creator and sustainer of all life, your life and mine, now and forever.
Became one of us, small, needy, dependent, a helpless babe. A child.
Holding nothing, grasping nothing, but his mother's hand and heart.

He the King of Glory, Christ the King, Savior of the World, came as a child. "For a child is born to us, a son is given to us. The government will rest on his shoulders.   And he will be called: Wonderful Counselor, Mighty God, Everlasting Father, Prince of Peace" (Isaiah 9:6).

Jesus tells his followers, and you and me, that unless we become like little children, we cannot enter the kingdom of heaven. I wonder what he means. What is it about being childlike that allows us to enter into the mystery of God's kingdom? Could it be we need the eyes, ears and faith of a child to see all of life with wonder, to live with the mystery of what is, and what isn't, to know we are loved and cared for even when we are small, needy, dependent and vulnerable?

Jesus told his disciples, "The Son can do nothing by himself. He does only what he sees the Father doing. Whatever the Father does, the Son also does. For the Father loves the Son and shows him everything he is doing" (John 5:19). As followers of Jesus, we too, are invited to live as he did, waiting with childlike hope and anticipation, as we eagerly watch for signs of God's presence in our world. We're called to live with childlike faith and joy as we receive all of life as streams of gifts, given to us, for us, for the life of the world, if only we have eyes to see, child eyes, seeing all of life with wonder and gratitude, proof of our Father's love and care.

The path is narrow, this life of following Jesus, it's hard to see where we are going, we frequently lose sight of Jesus, and it often feels as if we've lost our way. When this happens, we are invited to simply wait, trusting his ability to lead, more than our ability to follow. For we've been told a little child, the Christ child, shall lead us, lead us into a life of deeper intimacy with our heavenly Father. Lead us to experience his deep and constant love and care for us in spite of our mistakes, our need to be important, to prove ourselves and earn his love. To let go of trying to earn his love; so we can begin to believe the good news that we are already loved, not for what we do, but for who we are, whose we are.

We're invited to let life be simple, believing we have enough, are enough, just as we are. Bid to relax into Jesus' arms and let ourselves be cared for instead of being "careful." To live life simply being who we are, knowing whose we are. And if we aren't sure who we are, as most of us aren't, to allow ourselves the freedom to discover our true selves in Christ knowing the spaciousness of infinite possibility and surprise.

A child
Childlike faith
Simply living, living simply
Free to be who we are and whose we are
Free to make mistakes
To try new things
To simply show up and watch to see what Jesus is doing this day, every day,
in us and in our world.
To not have to lead the way or save the world.
That's his job not ours.
Our job is to simply show up
with all that we are and all that we have
our lives and hearts given to Jesus
the life of the world
for the sake of the world.
To give our love
nothing held back
not playing it safe in case things don't work out so well
or as we think they should.
That's what Jesus did isn't it?
He became small, simple, a child.
And lived a life of radical, simple faith and trust.
Dependent each day on his Father's love and care
Totally abandoned to his Father's will.

Can we who bear his likeness, who are called to bear the life and light of Jesus in our world, live any differently? Each day, we are invited to wait in eager anticipation, as Mary did, beckoned beyond where we are to a life of radical availability so the life of Jesus may be born anew, embodied, in our hearts and lives and world. Bid to abandon the state of constant anxiety and worry about

42

doing things right (as if we really could get it right anyway) to simply let go and let ourselves be cared for like a child. And so discover Jesus has already got it right, made us right. That's his job not ours.

I hope and pray that, you, too, will discover your belovedness as you embrace a life of childlike faith and trust. As you take the downward journey of letting go of trying to control your life in order to receive the life you've been given, accepting Jesus' invitation to live a life of a childlike faith, full of wonder, mystery, and joy. Created in love. Invited to simply share love and grace with reckless abandon with everyone everywhere.

Paula is a spiritual director, retreat facilitator, writer, wife, and mother of four grown sons. She is the founder and program director of Doorways Ministries, providing days of prayer, Ignatian retreats, and a nine-month program based on the Spiritual Exercises of St. Ignatius as ways of deepening our lives with Christ. She is also the city coordinator for the Ignatian Spirituality Project, a Jesuit organization dedicated to offering spiritual retreats inspired by Ignatian Spirituality to people experiencing homelessness.

WEDNESDAY. Ten Hail Marys and Two Our Fathers: Church as Correctional Institution.
Michael Carroccino

"Whatever you bind on earth will be bound in heaven, whatever you loose on earth will be loosed in heaven" (Matt. 16:19). In this first week of Advent, our scriptures and prayers mark the "great reversal": the coming of Jesus' reign and the time when all things are made right. All of us have a part to play in this great reconciliation to God and to one another, when evil is identified and cast out of creation such that we are no longer separated, but unified in Christ. As we prepare for God's coming, what can we do to "loose" ourselves and others from the shackles of conflict, division, and strife? Is there a way to live well and "be at peace with everyone" we reasonably can be (Rom. 12:18)?

We are not created to be free-floating, disconnected moral beings. Rather, every decision we make is a product of the commitments and relationships which claim us combined with an awareness of our place within the larger world. Are we always faithful to our commitments and relationships? Are we constantly aware of an overarching vision for the good of all creation? Hardly. And yet, we claim membership in a community whose self-described mission is the restoration of all people to unity with God and one another in Christ (*Book of Common Prayer*, 855).

How are we to faithfully allow such a mission to claim our lives in the face of such clear and common failure? The Bible tells us that if we confess our wrongdoing, God is faithful and just to forgive us (1 John 1:9). God's invitation is always beckoning, God's calling is always tugging from within, but the barriers to action in our learned behaviors and attitudes, in our weakness and despair, make the spiritual journey one fraught with hairpin turns and trails that peter out.

It has become a cinematic cliché to witness a confession ending with the priest doling out formulaic prayers of penance like my junior-high gym teacher doled out the punishment of push-ups or "writing lines" for poor behavior. "Twelve Our Fathers," he might intone, "and Eight Hail Marys," as if some magic recipe would somehow rectify the pain we have caused ourselves and others. But the cliché—as they so often disappointingly do—indicates a deeper truth: it is in the hands of the church, as in *all of us*, to address the pain of sin.

In the past generation, the rite of Confession was renamed the Rite of Reconciliation. This name change is instructive, as it implies a much more relational interaction, one of repair rather than simple dismissal. If the work of the church is restoration, perhaps the first place to start is within our worshipping community — by a regular practice of reconciling with God and one another. Prayers of confession are a regular part of Sunday worship for many Christians, but the Rite of Reconciliation offers the chance to take it one step further: the participants are invited to make an act of penance, a step in the right direction to repair the hurt their sin has caused (*Book of Common Prayer*, 447-452).

In the Middle Ages, penance took on an outsized character in Christian life, and, unfortunately, the very words associated with its practice still carry negative connotations: think about 'correctional' facilities, "penitent"-iaries, "reform"-atories, and so forth. But buried in the sensational accounts of self-flagellation and capital punishment was the essence of penitential practice: reform (as in, re-formation: repairing poorly formed habits and attitudes) for the individuals who agreed to specific reconciling actions under the care of a minister. Certainly there were abuses, especially when the church was conflated with the law of the land. But at the heart of penance lies a very much redeemable practice of intentional soul repair.

What might modern penance look like? Maybe a pastor or spiritual director will recommend marital counseling. Maybe someone will finally begin attending AA. Maybe a phone call will be made or letter written owning responsibility in a long-standing family conflict. Maybe the penitent will begin volunteering at a local organization that serves the population that previously received their acts of hatred. Perhaps we may even extend penance to restoring relationships with the environment or the economy by helping to clean up a polluted stream or beginning to purchase fair trade products.

The church devotes itself to the restoration of all to unity with God and one another. What we bind on earth will be bound in heaven. We cannot "jot and tittle" our way into right relationship, but we can confess, repent, and forgive one another. We can put ourselves in the path of evil when it is perpetrated upon the powerless, and we can work to counteract it in the structures of humanity. We can bind ourselves to one another in love. With the help of God and our sisters and brothers in Christ, we can set an intention this Advent to "loose" the hold of evil on our hearts. Given time and prayer, maybe—just maybe—the church can become a true correctional facility.

Michael serves as a priest at St. Mark's Episcopal Cathedral in Seattle. When not creating kitchen chaos in his quest for gastronomic bliss, he enjoys spending time in nature with his wife and two young children. More of his writing may be found in his and Kristin's forthcoming book Boats Without Oars: Ancient-Future Evangelism, An American Road Trip and Collected Stories from the Episcopal Church.

THURSDAY. Peace Dancing. *Esther Hizsa*

Peace is joy resting, and joy is peace dancing

—Charles Haddon Spurgeon

September 1998, I got a phone call from my brother. "She left me," he said and began to cry. As he filled in the details, a new reality unfolded, and there was no folding it back to the way things were before.

"I wish you weren't so far away," I said wiping the tears from my cheeks.

"Me too," he said. "I might need to call a lot."

"That's O.K. Call anytime," I replied.

Once or twice a week, my brother called. He'd talk and cry until he was too tired to say any more. And I'd listen, two thousand miles from his pain. Two months after his wife left, my brother went for counseling. He told me about the sessions when he called. I listened, fascinated by what I heard. But in one conversation, he asked me a question. All of a sudden it wasn't just about him anymore.

"The counselor asked me about our childhood," he said. "I told her I didn't remember Mom or Dad ever holding us. Do you? Do you remember them hugging us?"

Not one memory came to mind.

"The counselor thought that was sad."

"Hmm," I said and looked up to see my husband pointing at his watch. "Oh, man. It's 9:30! I'd better go or I'll be late for work. I love you." "I love you, too," he said. I grabbed my bag, kissed Fred goodbye and drove to East Vancouver through the slushy snow. At ten, I arrived for my sleepover shift at a group home for developmentally disabled adults.

I pushed the phone call from my mind and went about my duties. But when I climbed into bed, I thought about what my brother had said. There was no getting around it: though my parents did their best, my siblings and I did not receive the affection we longed for as children. The counselor's validation made me weep. And once I started to weep, I couldn't stop crying. Finally, I fell asleep with a song by Rich Mullins playing in my head:

47

"Hold me Jesus 'cause I'm shaking like a leaf

You have been King of my glory

Won't you be my Prince of Peace?"[13]

The next morning as I helped one of the residents pick out clothes for church, she asked me if I felt better. She must have heard me crying. Once I got home, there was the usual rush getting the kids fed and out the door. We arrived at church while the congregation was singing the first verse of "O Come, O Come Emmanuel." Behind us a woman came in with her family. She was carrying her four-month-old daughter in a car seat and set her down on the floor at the back of the church while she hung up her coat.

I crouched down in front of the baby and put on a smile. "I hear you're playing baby Jesus in this year's Christmas pageant," I said. "Feeling up to the part?"

The baby stared back at me with ancient eyes as if she, too, knew I was grieving. She curled her fingers around one of mine and looked at me. At that moment, it seemed as if she was holding me, as if she really was Jesus. I felt comforted. The mom thanked me for watching her daughter and joined her family in the sanctuary. I stood there savoring the joy resting inside me.

I remember that moment as if it were yesterday; the memory is as crisp and clear as Christmas Day. "I bring you good news of great joy," the angel told the shepherds that first Christmas. "The Savior has been born." The shepherds left their flocks and found baby Jesus wrapped in cloths, lying in a manger, and knelt down and worshiped him. They went home rejoicing, peace dancing in their souls. We, too, rejoice for Jesus has come into our world, into our lives, and into our grief with tidings of comfort and joy.

Esther Hizsa lives in Burnaby, B.C. with her husband Fred. They have two children and two grandchildren. Esther works part time as the associate pastor of New Life Community Church, has a Master of Divinity degree from Regent College, and is a trained spiritual director (SoulStream). But her first call is to writing. Her work has been published in the MB Herald, SoulStream *website and her blog,* An Everyday Pilgrim http://estherhizsa.wordpress.com.

---

[13] Rich Mullins, "Hold me Jesus." *A Liturgy, A Legacy & A Ragamuffin Band*, 1993.

FRIDAY. Let it Melt.
Joanna ES Campbell

I recently learned how to eat chocolate, just in time for Advent. All these years, peeling back the foil and gobbling a chocolate coin or a chocolate Santa seemed like natural holiday etiquette. Granted, this practice may be linked to the year my mom purchased Advent calendars with tiny chocolates behind each door. Being the preparer she is, she bought the Advent calendars months in advance. In that time, a leak developed in the roof of our home. Without anyone realizing, rainwater seeped into my parent's bedroom closet where my mom kept her holiday supplies tucked high out of reach from curious hands. The rainwater leaked onto the calendars and dried enough for my mom not to notice the damage. On the first day of Advent, my mom presented my brothers and me with the chocolate-filled calendars, and we couldn't have been more excited. I pried the paper door open, and plucked the chocolate out. The taste of mold was unmistakable. And yet, I couldn't resist. I needed to open each door each day. Even if I couldn't consume the entire piece, I wanted to take a small bite. I needed to taste just a little bit of Advent. Theo Chocolate in Seattle's Fremont neighborhood taught me how to eat chocolate. Theo's is the first organic, fair trade chocolate factory in the United States. The perky tour guide passed the varied chocolate samples around the room and instructed us to let the chocolate melt on our tongues. "If you chew your chocolate," she said, "then you're missing out on the bouquet." She's right. Have you ever just let the chocolate melt in your mouth? It's an exercise in anticipation. The rewards are great. Hints of cinnamon, cayenne, or citrus can blossom like moonflowers—their beauty takes you by surprise. Your eyes will widen. Flavors will arrive that you miss by crunching and swallowing. I liken the crunch/swallow method to guzzling homemade apple cider. If you're thirsty, drink a tall glass of water. If you want to savor and become enveloped by warm waves of subtlety, sip the cider, let the chocolate melt, and dwell in the full, present moment.

Theo's mission for Fair Trade includes more than just equitable wages for those who grow the cocoa beans and more than sustainable agriculture practices. Chocolate, like wine, bears a *terroir*, a taste of place. Cocoa beans grown in Ecuador have a different flavor profile from beans grown in the Congo. The soil, the air, the water, and the hands of those tending the plants shape the taste of chocolate. When I place the chocolate sample on my tongue, I am tasting a little bit of a hillside in Peru blended with stories due east of the Galapagos

Islands. I can't eat Theo chocolate now without wondering about green sea turtles or what the earth smells like in Central Africa.

However you fill your home with the holiday spirit, whether in the company of scented candles, cedar boughs, steamy mugs of cider, or calendars full of chocolate, may you rest in the unfolding flavors each day brings.

Joanna ES Campbell was born in Iowa, grew up in Little Rock, Arkansas, has a Master's of Science in Resource Conservation from University of Montana, is presently in the Creative Writing MFA program at Seattle Pacific University, and lives with her husband, Dennis, in the rectory of St. Clement Episcopal Church in Seattle, Washington.

FEAST OF ST. NICHOLAS.
December 6. St. Nicolas, *Sara Leigh*

I tiptoed out of my bedroom in the predawn hours to a lights-a-twinkle fragrant Christmas fir, eager to see what Santa had left for me. But the shag carpet beneath the tree was barren, even of the presents from the night before. Barren—except for a bundle of switches beneath it.

For a bad girl, the attached card said. I bawled angry, hurt tears. My father came out to the living room, and started laughing uproariously. *It was a joke,* he said. *Just a joke. Santa did it as a joke.* I looked up at the St. Nicholas doll that sat on the nearby wall clock and narrowed my eyes.

From that point on, I had a serious issue with Christmas in general, and St. Nick specifically. I was terrified of him, as well as resentful.

My family was run by two staunch atheists who warned us off of Jesus, yet every year, my parents pulled out "St Nicholas," a rosy-cheeked, white-haired doll, switches in one hand and a bag of gifts in another. Santa was real and always watching our behavior, our parents said. Switches weren't idle threats in my home, where physical punishment was severe and swift. *He sees you when you're sleeping/ he sees when you're awake,* my mother would sing throughout the year, which just added to the sense of dread and the idea that St. Nick was a bit of a creepy dude, overly concerned with children's ability to obey their parents.

Christmas day itself was a frenzy of present opening and comparisons—who did Santa/St. Nick like best out of the four children, after all? Finding out Santa wasn't "real" was nothing more than a relief.

As an adult, I've mostly avoided Christmas, downplaying the season with my own children, and telling them that Santa was fun, but not real. And yet this year, at Easter, I was baptized in the Episcopal Church, after accepting the honest truth that no, I didn't have all the answers, and I needed the help of God. One of the truest blessings of this journey has been the ability to regard situations with new eyes, with a curious mind and a vulnerable heart, secure in the knowledge that I am loved.

So the upcoming Christmas season stirs up a fire of anticipation, fear and inquisitiveness. I reinvestigated the story of St. Nicholas, that grinning gnome of my childhood, and discovered that far from being a fastidious child watcher, legends tell of a figure who is fiercely protective of children. These aren't heart-warming "Chicken Soup for the Soul" tales, either. For example, in one, St. Nicholas brings back to life children murdered by a butcher. He revives a baby left to die in a house fire, rescues a boy from kidnappers and anonymously provisions a dowry, so girls aren't sold into slavery. This St. Nicholas furiously cared for the rights of children.

Which stories are true? How did St. Nicholas, defender and miracle-worker for children, become the stick-and-carrot fellow that sat in my living room? I imagine, as with many things, the narrative changed to satisfy adults' needs and enforce social rules. It was convenient to deemphasize his protective nature, when one wants kids in bed by 8 p.m. In my family, it was to coerce us into desirable behavior.

It's not my place to verify truth or accuracy, but the stories we tell help define our lives we live today. This year, my husband, children and I will celebrate December 6, the traditional feast day of St. Nicholas. I've found alternatives to both how I was raised and mainstream Christian celebrations; a third way, as it were. We'll fill shoes with candies, fill our heart with prayers, and fill our tree with origami and handmade felt ornaments, and fill our stomachs with spice cookies shaped like St. Nicholas. I might even tell a not-so-scary tale or two about how St. Nicholas saved children. In any case, I will let the children know they are loved by my husband and me, St. Nicholas and God; there is no need to fear any one of us.

And on December 24, I will be in church, with a heart full of gratitude for the ability to look at old stories with new eyes, and retell them more completely.

Sara Leigh is a freelance journalist and mom to two kids based in Los Angeles who loves Fridays and eating store-bought pastries.

SATURDAY. *Gather, Feast, Create*

Gather

The first week of Advent is coming to a close. If you are keeping an Advent wreath, you may decide to go ahead and light the second Advent candle at your gathering on this evening. Beginning a religious "feast" at sundown is a traditional way to celebrate. This is also the gathering to celebrate St. Nicholas. In some countries, gifts are exchanged on St. Nicholas Day and not Christmas, and much pageantry is involved in the celebration. A simpler way to celebrate would be to have guests, especially any children who are present, leave their shoes outside the door to be mysteriously filled with chocolate coins and oranges as St. Nicholas passes by, or perhaps St.

Nicholas will even pay a visit to the gathering and share some of his favorite stories. Over dinner, your group might discuss reconciliation, peace-making, and justice, all attributes Nicholas of Myra (St. Nicolas) was known for, and how they may be lived out during the next week. The website *www.stnicholascenter.org* is an excellent resources for ideas.

Feast

Meal: Mediterranean foods potluck

St. Nicholas lived in Myra, now part of Turkey, so this week's feast enjoys cuisine from that part of the world. In addition to recipe suggestions found in the Appendices, consider trying dolmades, spanakopita, Greek salad, rice, baklava, and any other Mediterranean dishes that come to mind. Many of these may be found at local markets, but are also fun to prepare if you have the time.

Create

This week's O Antiphon reminds us that the "Sacred Lord of Israel is the only joy of every human heart." Writers this week have encouraged us to think about reconciliation, justice, and peace. One activity this week is to consider writing letters as a group to government officials encouraging fair and just decisions and lawmaking. Many websites, such as www.contactingthecongress.org in the United States, list addresses for officials. Letters could be shared aloud after dinner, and one person might volunteer to put them in the mail. Another idea for this evening would be to reflect as a group on one of the stories of St. Nicholas' ministry (paying the daughters' dowries anonymously or speaking out for his convictions at the Council of Nicea are two such stories that come to mind) and respond with individual drawings or writing to hang up at home and contemplate.

—Kristin

O RADIX JESSE

"O Flower of Jesse's stem you have been raised up as a sign for all peoples; kings stand silent in your presence; the nations bow down in worship before you. Come, let nothing keep you from coming to our aid."

Week Two of Advent

[Image: People gather to draw water from a well in India.]

O Root of Jesse

In the second week of Advent we are reaching the middle of the season. Perhaps the luster and excitement of the first Sunday of Advent is beginning to wear thin; the prospect of completing things that remain to be done before the first day of Christmas feels daunting, at best. Here is a liminal space, an opening in which we stand with one foot on either side of a threshold. On one side, we could be swept away by the flood of parties, final exams, finding the perfect gift for the unappeasable person, and addressing holiday greeting cards. On the other, we could become stoic and cynical, angry at all "those" people who don't seem to understand the "real reason for the season" with all of their exuberant caroling and endless demands for yet another dozen cookies for their various parties. If we attempt the middle way and embrace liminality, we might persevere in the tension of the almost-but-not-quite, with our gaze alternating between the past and the future, but working hard to remain in what *this* moment offers.

People in many countries around the world mark time during Advent and Christmas with a nativity set. St. Francis of Assisi is said to have crafted the first set of figures representing Biblical scenes written about the birth of Jesus as a way to convey the wonder and power of Christ's Incarnation to people of all ages, many of whom were illiterate. In our home, an empty wooden stable, the one I used as a child that has miraculously survived my own children's early years, is placed on a table in the living room with just a few sheep and the old cow. Baby Jesus is hidden away until Christmas morning. Mary, Joseph, and the donkey, as well as the three kings, begin their travels across the different rooms of our house, hoping to arrive by Christmas Eve and Epiphany, respectively. In parts of France, nativity figures are more diverse; clay "santons" (saints) who visit the manger include bakers, policemen, craftsmen, a washer woman, and many others representing the truth that *everyone* is welcome to worship the newly born Christ.[14]

Our O Antiphon this week reminds us that Jesus was "raised up as a sign for *all* peoples" and that kings stand silent and nations bow down before him. We implore Christ to "come, let nothing keep you from coming to our aid." The writers featured in this week's readings invite us to stand in that uncomfortable, liminal place of realizing that though we may be part of the privileged middle-class world who fret over which blend of Cashmere sweater or vintage wine to

---

[14] Barbara Beckwith. "Santons and Their Christmas Lessons," http://www.americancatholic.org/Messenger/Dec2004/Feature1.asp. The full article appears in Appendix C.

purchase for our beloved, countless individuals across the globe face a very different reality.

In our Advent waiting, we must wake up and remember that our choices *matter*, that the ways we spend our money, time, and prayers have a profound impact on the lives of people we may never meet, who often look and act in ways that we would like to ignore and forget. We become the hands and feet of Christ and seek to answer the calls of the oppressed to "come, let nothing keep *you* from coming to *our* aid."

—Kristin

Prayer for Week Two of Advent

In this season of waiting,
breathe in life.

Life of the One
who created all things,
whose image we bear.

In this season of waiting,
breathe in love.

Love of the One
who gave a precious Son
to live as one of us.

In this season of waiting,
breathe in peace.

Peace of the One
who calmed the sea
and quiets the tumult of our souls.

In this season of waiting
breathe in hope.

Hope that the One
for whom we wait
is indeed making all things whole.
—Christine

FEAST OF THE IMMACULATE CONCEPTION. December 8. Maryam.
Mary Keenan

Recently, I met with an interfaith group of women—half Muslim and half Christian—to study Mary/Maryam in the Quran. My participation came as kind of a fluke—another woman in the group had to drop out, so a friend invited me to fill in. But it touches so many things I am interested in that I could not resist. And, you know, *Mary*. I need no other reason.

I knew that Mary was important in Islam, but our first meeting reminded me just how much. She is not only the mother of Jesus—a major prophet in Islam—but the only woman mentioned by name in the entire Quran.

Each woman introduced herself to the group by saying what they most admired about Mary, each coming from her own tradition and life experience. Without exception, the Muslim women cited Mary's chastity and strength as her most admirable qualities. The Christian women had a bit more variety, but tended more towards strength, bravery, and loyalty. Our inspiration is most certainly rooted in our own scriptural traditions.

The stories about Mary have common elements in Islam and Christianity, but they are not the same. Right from the beginning, some differences in belief and tradition surprised us. Mary lived in the Temple? And gave birth under a date palm tree? Say what?! No, she was a poor woman from a backwater town. And she married a guy named Joseph. Really! You can read what the Quran and the New Testament report about Mary pretty easily on the Internet. But what you won't get are the individual expressions—verbal and facial expressions—as women meeting face to face try to articulate just what it is about Mary that stays with us. She is regarded simultaneously with awe and affection. Women, particularly mothers, identify with her sacrifice and loss in a culture and conflict that is dominated by men. In Islam, she is an isolated figure who lived in a cell at the Temple, away from everyone but an uncle. In Christianity, she is often depicted in art as solitary and absorbed in her own thoughts. Yet in both traditions, her most important role is undeniably physical and fleshy —the birth of her son.

Over the course of four weeks, we read passages from the Quran and discussed their significance, as well as contrasting those passages with her portrayal in the

Christian Bible. Our various beliefs and traditions about Mary were quite different in some respects, yet there was something about this long-ago Mary that caught our attention and kept it: she accepted the unexpected—a pregnancy, a miraculous child, a public life—with grace.

During Advent, Mary is center stage for Christians. We watch her ride across our Advent calendars and crèches toward Bethlehem for her part in a familiar story. The story is, in fact, so familiar that I wonder if we take for granted how peculiar and strong and dynamic Mary must have been. So impressive, in fact, that she is a central figure in the faith of Islam, which developed seven centuries later, and stays with both traditions today.

At our last meeting, our group of women reflected on our discussions about Mary, what was most important to us about her. And it occurred to us that Mary is very often presented as an ideal woman or a role model for women—but why only for women? Her life, her character, and her relationship with God are instructive for any person of faith, not just women. There was a noticeable energy in the room as we began to name the many ways that Mary's life is inspiring—and noticed how her example was equally applicable to all believers. She is brave, faithful, virtuous, and attentive to God's will for her.

It is clear in both the Koran and the Bible that Mary is a person who DID inspire both men and women. It is equally clear that, over the centuries, her example has habitually been relegated to women. Our group parted with the goal of reminding our communities of faith about the powerful story and person of Mary. After all, our own study taught us that if Mary's life inspired saints and prophets from Joseph to Mohammed, there must be plenty more for all of us to learn. [15]

Mary Keenan lives in Austin, Texas, with two kids, a husband, and a dog. She has an M.Div. from Yale Divinity School and loves to think theologically about almost everything. She also loves metaphors, tangents, and rabbit trails and where they lead. Among her thousands of jobs, she is a teacher, preacher, strategic planner, grant writer, fundraiser, and writer. She blogs at maryology.com.

---

[15] Editor's note: Many countries and faith traditions celebrate the "immaculate conception of Mary." The conception being celebrated is that of Mary by her mother Ann, not that of Jesus. Both Christians and Muslims dedicate this day to Mary's conception.

SUNDAY. Advent, Children, Justice, Wonder, and Humility. *Steve Wickham*

The Saviour's birth was the humblest of beginnings:

"Mary gave birth to her firstborn son and wrapped him in bands of cloth, and laid him in a manger, because there was no place for them in the inn (Luke 2:7, New Revised Standard Version)."

The Westernized Christmas, paradoxically, is very much a children's event. Despite negative allusions from the onerously pious, there is much to be gleaned about why Christmas is so exciting for children. Recalling my childhood, Christmases are about redeeming long-cherished memories of waiting, hoping, praying for wishes to come true—not just materialistic wishes, either.

The Salubrious Wonder in Advent

The celebration of the coming of the Incarnation-of-God into the world is history's hinging point. The God-fearing Jews had waited ever-so-patiently for the coming of the prophesied Saviour. The promised King approached, and then came in the person of Jesus. Hundreds of years passed before the Lord arrived. And in all the anticipation wonder grew. Advent seemed to tarry, but it never more surely arrived right on time!

We think, in our day, perhaps days after Christmas, "Oh well, Christmas is over again for another year," and often we are relieved—the burden of preparations is over; a family event has been accomplished; the stress is now over (for another year)!

Maybe we forget the wonder in Advent, for a child thinks differently. They wait patiently all year, enjoy their Christmas, and even lament the coming and the passing of a terrific celebration of joy, peace, love, and hope. We don't know if the child is excited because it is the celebration of the coming of God into the world. It probably isn't.

But there is clarity of spiritual coolness in the wonder that this season generates. As an adult I find myself hankering for those childhood times, where birthdays and Christmases meant something more intrinsically wondrous.

The wonder that children can experience as Advent approaches, regardless of the materialism attached, is a resplendent watch point for parents and other adults alike. To know joy is to know the sense of wonder that a child experiences in contemplating the mystery in the replete, yet perfectly safe, unknown.

Wonder, Excitement, Humility, and Making a Difference
As we reflect over this joy that a child experiences in the approach of this season, there is the opportune time to teach the child through the narrative of their unfolding lives.

Never better may there be an opportunity to connect our children to advocacy for the social justice issues Jesus himself would grieve over. We get out our world maps and we wonder aloud. We enjoy with inclusivity the diversity over our green earth. And, in that, we commit to helping those less fortunate. We want to know their plight! We want our children to grow within their hearts a yearning for God's justice to sweep the world. We want a better tomorrow.

There are the acts of random kindness we can commit to—one a day over the season of Advent—as we count the days down from the fourth Sunday before December 25.

Expressions of humility and selflessness come in one-million-and-one colours of thoughtful and behavioural expression. Such humility and selflessness are things our children will just soak up. In this they will know Jesus.

Whatever we plan, we plan better when we keep our kids engaged. Advent presents many opportunities for object lessons, in converting our children's ambient joy into the Joy of the Lord.

Advent, most of all, celebrates the coming of the King of Kings and Lord of Lords in such a way that we acknowledge he is coming again!

Waiting patiently through Advent, as children wait, anticipating the movement of God in our hearts, is our blessed opportunity. If we experience justice, let us fight injustice. If we experience wonder, let us conquer ambivalence. If we experience humility, we let that seed germinate and rest in our souls, forever.

Most of all, let us share these experiences with our children.

Steve is a regular contributor to Godspace *from Perth, Australia. He is a Baptist pastor who holds degrees in science, divinity, and counseling. He blogs at* Epitome *and* Tribework.

MONDAY. Gritty Peacemakers.
Meredith Griffin

"...Despite all the evidence that seems to be to the contrary, there is no way that evil and injustice and oppression and lies can have the last word."
—Desmond Tutu

As I write, unthinkable headlines are crossing our newspapers and television screens: *ISIS Systematically Beheading Children, Ferguson Police Move in to Disperse Protestors, Smoke Over Gaza as Israeli Palestinian Ceasefire Ends, Ebola Outbreak Like Wartime, Communities Protest Surge of Immigrant Children.*

Do you feel as overwhelmed as I do? As we begin to process one headline, another erupts. We watch, heartbroken. Then the reality that we are talking about *real* people and *real* families actually *living* these headlines sinks in. We are floored. And the scariest part of all? As Christians, we know Christ calls us to respond. *Okay God*, we say. *How about sending some money over to relief efforts in these various countries? I will pray. And I will definitely watch the news and talk about the headlines with people.* Yet, we are left dissatisfied. We wonder how much of an impact one person can really make. The need is far too great and let's face it, we still have to take out the trash and feed the dog. We helplessly watch and wait for resolution, hoping somehow the chaos will work itself out.

During Advent, retail stores fill their aisles with Christmas-themed merchandise featuring the phrase, "Peace on Earth." Christmas songs singing of peace can be heard on radio stations the day after Thanksgiving. Advent takes place during a cultural season that asks us to be celebratory, to promote peace and generosity. Yet, this supermarket version of peace can be mistaken for a sort of fuzzy emotion that deserves special attention during the holidays. Despite our best efforts to block them out, the sickening headlines continue to loom, even during Advent. We long to act; to find a way to heal the world of its pain and erase the anxiety it provokes within us, but we are left clueless. The problem lies in our first move. We instinctually begin with the question, *what are we supposed to do?*

In his book, *Peacework*, Henri Nouwen challenges us to move beyond the fuzzy, supermarket version of peace to a vocational peace. Unlike particular vocations, where some of us are called to be poets and others are called to be office clerks, it is a vocation for all. It is a way of *being*, a position we assume. We are to radiate and promote a *gritty* peace; a peace that doesn't always make us feel good, but that causes a sweaty brow and leaves dirt under our fingernails. The first step as peacemakers is not to first ask ourselves, *what are we supposed to do?* Instead, we first ask, *what posture do I take as I interact with a hostile world?* Once we've cultivated our vocation as peacemakers, when chaos breaks lose, we are ready to act.

What does it mean to cultivate our vocation as peacemakers? As peacemakers, we *act out of faith*. Have you ever noticed after performing miracles, many times Jesus tells the newly healed to "Go in peace"? Or in times of despair and awe, Jesus comforts his disciples with "Peace be with you"? Those who are healed (whether it be from a sickness or from their own sin) are told that it is their *faith* that has healed them. Once oppressed, the healed are now able to re-enter into the world, covered in God's peace. The disciples, grieved when Jesus tells them one day he will be leaving, still hold faith in Jesus' promise that he will send "another Counselor." The disciples' faith in Jesus' promise provides them the peace they so desperately need for God's appointed work. To "go in peace," we, too, must first see and be healed by God. Only then can we assume the faith needed to fuel our peacemaking. It is a faith that is renewed often, as we strive to see God all around us, daily. It is a faith that holds fast to a love that is stronger than any daunting headline.

Peacemakers are *brave*. We are brave because we have experienced peace in our own lives. The woman who had been bleeding for twelve years reached out to touch Jesus' robe because she believed even a small encounter with God could cure her. The woman's courage was her ticket to mystical participation with God, and in turn, peace. With both confidence and vulnerability, the woman made her move. Once healed, Jesus instructed the woman to "go in peace." The woman could then take the vocation of peacemaker, for she had encountered God's peace for herself. The woman shows us that to be a peacemaker, we embrace *humility*. Is there peace within our own homes? How about peace within our own communities? How might we expect to promote peace in the world if we do not act as peacemakers in our own personal lives? Mother Teresa was known to say, "What can you do to promote world peace? Go home and love your family." Being brave peacemakers means being brave enough to ask for forgiveness and to forgive. It means holding reconciliation in higher esteem than self-interest.

Peacemakers are *present*. We are present by entering into the solitude of prayer, which is an act of protest against a world of aggression and destruction. We are present as we participate in the ebb and flow of the liturgical calendar and in the seasons nature brings. We are present as we take the Eucharist each week, becoming the body of Christ we ingest. Being peacemakers is not a somber role, but can be a joyful one. We are joyfully present, especially during the Advent season as we wait in eager expectation on the birth of a new baby. This week includes the three-day fiesta and feast day of Our Lady of Guadalupe, which is most famously marked by bright pink and red Castile roses and celebratory dance. Even, and perhaps most often, it is in these times of great joy that we can be the most present and as a result, the most effective peacemakers. Our dancing is a sign to the world that God brings us hope for peace.

Finally, as peacemakers, we are *patient*. December is a dark time of year. This week also brings Saint Lucy's feast day, which is celebrated in many European and Eastern countries by a festival of light on the winter solstice, the shortest day of the year. One Croatian custom calls for families to plant a few grains of wheat in a small pot on the solstice. The family is to wait patiently for the sprouts to appear by Christmas, so they may place the pot by the nativity scene, signifying the "staff of life" and the nourishment of the Eucharist. As peacemakers, we are aware that darkness lies all around us. Wars are always being fought and illness continues to ensue. However, God calls us out of the darkness and into hope by telling us to plant seeds of peace, whether in our own homes or in a war-torn country. In anticipation of new beginnings, we wait patiently for our seeds to sprout, for the new baby Christ to be born.

Brave, present, and patient we do the gritty, but joyful work of peacemaking. We wait in eager expectation because at one time or another, we have experienced God's healing and peace in our own lives. We know the power in the peace we have found in God doesn't hold a candle to the world's violence. Although the world might be dark as we wait on life, we remember the wise words of Desmond Tutu who said, "We can never give up on anyone because our God was one who had a particularly soft spot for sinners." Now it's time to let God move through us as we embark on our vocation as peacemakers. As you decipher your own specific steps as a peacemaker, be creative. Let me know what you dream up.

Meredith lives on Galveston Island in Texas. She enjoys spending time outdoors with her husband and two young children. She holds a Bachelors degree in English Literature and Education as well as a Masters in Counseling from the Episcopal Seminary of the Southwest.

TUESDAY. Simplify and Celebrate: What Makes for a Better Christmas, a Better World? *Christine Sine*

Christmas is coming. We know it well because all the demons of consumerism and materialism have reared their ugly heads all around us. Most of us find ourselves in a real bind. Do we have a gift-free Christmas and turn our backs entirely on consumerism? Do we buy only gifts that come from fair trade, slave-free, or local organizations and feel that we are making difference with our purchases? Or do we develop a holier-than-thou attitude and turn our backs completely on the secular celebration of the season?

If we are honest, most of us struggle with these issues and are not sure how to enter into the true spirit of Christmas without disappointing our kids or denying our own enjoyment of Christmas goodies and unexpected presents. *Simplify Christmas, Celebrate Christ* we tell ourselves while hoping that we will find a Kindle Fire, or new camera under the tree.

For most of us, our simplification of Christmas is a compromise that hopefully does focus more on the celebration of the birth of Christ than on the secular materialistic spirit of the season. If you are struggling with these issues here are some thoughts for reflection.

Watch videos from *A New American Dream* (www.newdream.org) or *The Advent Conspiracy* (www.water.cc/advent) and reflect on the values that underlie your Christmas expenditures. Is Christ truly at the center of your celebrations? Consider making some of the changes suggested in the videos.

Delay your celebration of Christmas by celebrating Advent and the season of waiting in the days leading up to Christmas. I find that when I truly enter into the spirit of Advent that Christmas shopping is no longer enjoyable.

Simplify Christmas: Consider some of the ideas on the *Becoming Minimalist* website (http://www.becomingminimalist.com/simple-christmas-links/) on how to simplify life during this season.

Consider alternative celebrations to the usual Christmas parties. Former MSA team member Cindy Todd made soap for an event at Church of the Beloved in Edmonds, Washington, whose theme was "A Slave Free Christmas." It highlighted making or buying articles that were made without slave labour.

Participants also watched and talked about the film *Dreams Die Hard* and talked about the issues of slavery still present in the United States.

Consider paying more for less when you buy gifts. Tom and I are Christmas people and, to be honest, could not really imagine exchanging no gifts at Christmas, but we do restrict our gift giving and try to buy locally produced or fair trade items as much as possible. And that does not mean that we restrict our giving to coffee and chocolate either. There is a growing array of stores that provide fairly traded gifts in everything from clothing to soccer balls.

Consider alternative charitable gifts to organizations like World Concern and Heifer Project that provide animals and other gifts for people in impoverished communities to enable them to start small businesses.

Give away one day's wages to an organization of your choice, like One Day's Wages (www.onedayswages.org) that works to overcome poverty.

Christine Sine is the Executive Director of Mustard Seed Associates. She trained as a physician in Australia and developed the medical ministry for Mercy Ships. She now speaks on issues relating to changing our timestyles and lifestyles to develop a more spiritual rhythm for life. She has authored several books including Return to Our Senses: Reimagining How We Pray; Godspace: Time for Peace in the Rhythms of Life; *and* Tales of a Seasick Doctor. *Christine blogs at* http://godspace-msa.com.

FEAST OF OUR LADY OF GUADALUPE.
December 12. A Letter to Mary. *Jessie Smith*

Growing up Episcopalian I always thought Mary was not for us, that Mary was for the Catholics. But over the years, I have learned that is not true and I started to spend time with Mary. I keep meeting her in different ways and places. Now, I talk to her.

This week I wanted to preach a sermon full of information about Mary: who she was and is, traditions of Mary around the world, and tell you about my own relationship with her. But the spirit moved in another way. Today, I am going to read you a letter I wrote to Mary this week.

Dear Mary,

I'm coming to you today because I know you can handle it. You are the mother of God, the woman God saw fit to help Jesus bear the weight of this world. Mary, I am writing to you because you are fierce, you are tough, your heart is pierced, still bleeding and yet you love. I'm coming to you because I know you are still hanging around God's people. I have heard it said, and I agree, Mary, that you "appear in times that are not calm, and in clouds of dust that are not particularly picturesque." I've heard it said, you come, Mary "skidding to sudden stop in dark cars on uneven darker gravel roads." Mary, you "stand at every street corner, even those where it seems that maybe even God herself ought to be cautious." Mary, I think I need you or some of your strength to show up in the midst of this "mud, dirt, storms and thunder of life."[16]

See, things are pretty rough down here right now: Palestine, Ukraine, Iraq, Isis, Zionism, Ebola…it goes on and on. But here, closer to home we have a problem and I thought—no I felt—that you could do what you do and love us through this problem.

Mary, last week, a boy was shot. In Ferguson, Missouri, a young unarmed African American man, with his hands in the air, backing away from the cops, stating he had no gun. Michael Brown was shot not once, but seven times. His death is tragic enough, but the thing is Mary, this happens all the time.

---

[16] Clarissa Pinkola Estés, *Untie the Strong Woman: Blessed Mother's Immaculate Love for the Wild Soul* (Sounds True, 2011), 270.

This week, our news channels, and feeds, have been filled with stories and challenges to face the reality of racial injustice. Mary, I want to admit it: I too often forget the privilege I walk through this world with. **I pretend this world is the way I think it should be.**

Mary I want to tell you about this experience; two weeks ago, I was driving home from church [still wearing my priest's collar], I was singing along to Patty Griffin blaring on the radio, [my dog] Jonas's head was way out the window, tongue flapping in the wind. I noticed the cars around me slowing down and staring. It took me a couple of minutes to realize a cop was following me. Actually his lights were on, and he had been trying to pull me over.

I quickly pulled to the side of the road. I haven't been pulled over in years, and although I am a fan of watching the show "COPS," I still did what you are not supposed to do. I turned off the car and started getting out of the driver's seat to approach the police car.

The officer asked me to get back inside the car, and then apologized because "he didn't realize who he was pulling over."

It turned out, he pulled me over because my registration was expired and wouldn't you know, no matter how much I stumbled through my purse and shuffled around my glove box, I couldn't find updated insurance info either.

In light of Michael Brown's death and the riots in Ferguson this week, another young man, Alex Landau, retold his story. In 2009, Landau, then a college student, was stopped by Denver police for making an illegal turn. Some assumptions about this upper middle-class African American man were made. The officer saw him as every black man that ever committed a crime. After questioning the officer's right to search his car without a warrant, Landau was severely beaten.[17]

So how did my traffic stop end? Well, the officer went back to his car to run my plates. Even though I told the officer I had probably just forgotten to put the tabs on my car, it turns out my registration was expired several months ago. He offered me some friendly advice about putting reminders on my iphone and

---

[17] NPR Staff, "After A Traffic Stop, Teen Was 'Almost Another Dead Black Male," Aug. 15, 2014 www.npr.org/2014/08/15/340419821/after-a-traffic-stop-teen-was-almost-another-dead-black-male.

because he "didn't want to get in trouble with the man Upstairs," he did not write me a ticket for the expired registration and failing to carry proof of insurance.

My privilege feels like a slap in the face. It is a wake-up call. It is too easy to forget ourselves. Especially living in the Pacific Northwest, it is easy for those of us not targeted, to forget or ignore the reality of racism and stereotyping.

And I know this is not just a problem with cops, Mary, we have a bigger problem than that: our racism is systemic. Infection has run rampant and the body has even begun to normalize the causalities.

Mary, I was down [in Portland] on Glisan, Friday afternoon. I came out of Winco [grocery store] and sat and watched people come and go. There was so much more color and diversity in that parking lot then I see most days living in the Pacific Northwest. I watched mothers with gaggles of kids in tow and feet shuffling behind walkers and part of my heart was pierced.

In the face of diversity, I could feel within myself deeply ingrained prejudices. I could feel with each breath the racism that is ingrained in me and I hated it and prayed to God to be healed, to be released because this week America is remembering that our problem with racism isn't just uncle so-and-so's inappropriate comments at Thanksgiving. The real racism walks the streets, lurks in alley ways, wears a police uniforms, approves and denies bank loans, and doesn't see you waiting at the counter. The real racism isn't just a word that starts with 'n' or bad jokes, the real racism that we are only beginning to face, has made this world unsafe for young black men to drive down the street. And Mary, I know in the depths of my heart, protected by my ignorance, there are still so many shards of racism. Like a broken drinking glass, it isn't a fully functional system of racism within me, but those jagged pieces of glass that are littered all over still hurt.

Mary, I know I can't be the only one. The real racism within me, although buffered by my education, my Christian love and liberal ideals is toxic. So what am I to do? What are we to do with a society littered with shards of racism? Mary, I know we have our work cut out for us. That is why I am writing to you.

Mary, you have always been strong enough to expose your heart to allow your soul to magnify God, to proclaim the release of the captives and the raising up of the lowly.

I suppose part of our task is to name the broken places and proclaim God's dominion over them. The least we can do, individually and as a community is to look our racism in the face and name it (even if it is subtle, safely hidden and seemingly benign). But our task is so much more than speaking into existence the world we want to be a reality. We know what we are to do: Pay attention to what is happening in the world and spend some time within ourselves in self examination, and most importantly listen (and believe), the voices of those who suffer and educate ourselves.

Mary, I have heard it said that you long ago gave up the pale blue virgin gig, now you lead a girl gang in heaven. Yes, you are still "serene, like a great ocean is serene." You are "obedient, like the sunrise is obedient to the horizon line."[18] I've heard that now you show off your strength, your ripped arms and muscular back that have carried so much weight for us.

Arms that have planted the roses of your love where they are most needed: in the dirt of oppression, poverty and grime. You plant your roses among barbed wire and blackberry vines, next to someone's cardboard bed under the bridge. Your roses grow in neglected playgrounds, under the feet of drug dealers. Your love grows through the concrete of our broken justice system. Your love grows despite the broken glass of our racism. Your love grows where it is most needed: around the causalities of our ignorance.

Mary, we need your strength. It is hard to speak up. Rachel Held Evans wrote: "To be honest, I'm scared—of saying the wrong thing, of revealing my ignorance, of detracting attention from the voices that really ought to be heard."[19] It was here, Mary, that I was challenged to take steps beyond grief and guilt. Evans wrote these words on her blog:

> [to] show solidarity with the oppressed, and challenge the privileged…
> **Well, that means challenging myself.**
> To listen better.
> To educate myself.
> **To remain open to correction.** (That one's hard!)
> To speak up, even when it's risky.
> To confront my own privilege, even when it's uncomfortable.

---

[18] Estés, 280.
[19] Rachel Held Evans, "On Race, The Benefit of the Doubt, and Complicity," *Rachelheldevans.com* (blog), 2014, http://rachelheldevans.com/blog/ferguson-race-benefit-of-the-doubt-complicity.

And to actually *believe* that racism is real and pervasive—present not only in the power structures of the Empire, or in the conversation around a neighboring table at a restaurant, but also in the dark corners of my own, dangerously-biased heart.

Lord, have mercy. Forgive us our sins. Light the path to change.[20]

Mary, Mother of God, Mother of Light in this world: you can nurture in the midst of it all and that is why I write to you today. I'm writing to you because I know you can handle it—stick it out with us as only a mother would do. Right now, we could use your presence: I want to study your ability to hold sorrow in your arms, watch the light in your son's eyes fade and still give out nothing but love.

Mary, I have heard it said that you grow your strongest roses in "the earthy ground, amongst horns honking, ambulances careening, children crying, out alternatively in joy and pain, all the people groaning and dancing and making love, every which way of humanity."[21] We need all the help we can get, with God, the Holy Spirit and our Savior, your son. Join us, Mary, in the mess of our brokenness and teach us to clean up what we have shattered, the shards of racism scattered in and around us.

Faithfully, your sister, your wanna-be gang member, and admirer,

Jessie.

Jessie is the vicar of St. Anne's Episcopal Church in Washougal, Washington. She lives nearby with her dog Jonas.

---

[20] Evans.
[21] Estés, 270.

Full text of Clarissa Pinkola Estés' poem from her book *Untie the Strong Woman*:

Coda: Mi Guadalupe is a
Girl Gang Leader in Heaven

Mi Guadalupe is a girl gang leader in Heaven.
She is unlike the pale blue serene woman.
She is serene, yes, like a great ocean is serene.
She is obedient, yes, like the sunrise
is obedient to the horizon line.
She is sweet, yes,
Like a huge forest of sweet maple trees.
She has a great heart, vast holiness,
and like any girl gang leader ought,
substantial hips.

Her lap is big enough
to hold every last one of us.
Her embrace
can hold us,
All.
And with Such Immaculate Love.

Aymen

(as my grandmother would say),
and a little woman.[22]

---

[22] Estés, 280.

FEAST OF ST. LUCY. December 13. Darkness and Light. *Kimberly Miller*

Despite the youth and beauty found at the center of the Feast of Saint Lucy traditions,[23] the story behind Saint Lucia of Syracus, whom today's Feast of Saint Lucy celebrates, is deeply disturbing.

My first god-daughter's name is Lucy. Her namesake is the Saint Lucia of Syracus. I knew nothing about the Feast of Saint Lucy or of Lucia of Syracus when I set about writing this devotional last summer. I called Lucy's mom and asked her to tell me more about the Feast of Saint Lucy. Accurate or not, her description that warm summer night brought visions of a crisp December evening, a candlelit church, a choir chanting The Holly and the Ivy, and young, barefooted girls in simple white dresses wearing crowns of laurel. The Feast is a celebration of feminine youth, light, and alludes to the bride of Christ.

However, the more I read about Saint Lucy, who was born in the late 3rd century and lived as a subject of the Roman empire, the visions of innocence and beauty were replaced by tragic images of unbridled hatred, dogma, betrayal, incomprehensible injustice, torture, persecution, forced prostitution, and a young woman whose only leverage against vicious public policies was to perpetrate violence upon her own body.

Lucy was killed in 304 at the peak of the "Diocletianic Persecution" where intolerance of the Christian religion had reached a fever pitch. Where Hitler implemented "the final solution" attempting to eradicate the Jews, so the Diocletian Emperors issued a series of violent and repressive "edicts against the Christians" aimed at terminating every believer in the realm. Throughout the empire, Christians were being put to death in violent and degrading scenarios.

As the story goes, Lucy, having committed her life to the service of Christ, refused to enter into an arranged marriage with a pagan. The jilted bridegroom betrayed her identity as a Christian to the local governing body. According to legend the local authorities meant to sell her into prostitution as punishment.

---

[23] Editor's Note: St. Lucy is traditionally honored by the young women in a church or the oldest daughter in a family wearing a crown of candles and serving the family breakfast or singing and processing at a church service honoring her. These symbols of light and service honor the legend that Lucy would enter the dark catacombs and bring sustenance to the Christian prisoners.

Lucy's unimaginable recourse was to gouge out her own eyes and was subsequently put to death.

Of course, while Lucy's story is tragic, it is an exception. That is why she is a venerated Saint. Most lives are meant to be lived, not sacrificed in death and martyrdom. You and I will likely never face the profound injustice young Lucy was overwhelmed by. Ultimately, her story inspires me to continue choosing to live, really live, as an acknowledgement of God's gift of Breath. Beset by occasional severe depression, I intimately understand that living is all about choice.

Today I choose life! I will pick up my heart from the threshing floor, where it has been crushed and prepared, and I will again give it to the world in full recognition that I cannot keep it safe. In fact, how would I love, live, and create today if I weren't willing to risk the inevitability that everything beautiful, powerful, and life-giving comes from the loss of just those qualities? I will find my purpose today, like I did yesterday, like I will again tomorrow. And I will do this with my eyes open, with my heart threshed, and my losses sown back into the earth, as if something good may grow from each one.

Kimberly works a mental health therapist in the greater-Seattle area. She also lives with a severe mental illness and so uses her professional as well as her personal experience to advocate for consumer rights and systemic change in the mental health system. She graduated with a Masters of Arts in Counseling Psychology from The Seattle School of Theology & Psychology in 2005. She finds solace and outlet in gardening, writing, her family, backpacking and hiking, outdoor photography, and her three adorable dogs.

WEDNESDAY. Spending, Ethics, and Justice in a Globalized World. *Chris Heuertz*

One of today's most complicated moral issues is how to spend money responsibly in a globalized world.

I'm as conflicted as the next person about it. I love coffee, for example, but I'm not a fan of fair-trade coffee, because frankly, I rarely find an excellent cup of it.

I'm deeply troubled by child labor and sweatshops, but I still don't make my own clothes. I don't know how, and even if I did, I honestly wouldn't have time to do it.

Some of our most lucrative oil companies are among the world's greatest human-rights abusers, but I don't drive a hybrid car, because they are still too expensive.

Finally, I would love to buy all my produce locally, but I live in Omaha, Nebraska. Enough said.

For years, I've wrestled with these issues. I've read books that offer hopeful promises and gimmicky solutions—most of them filled with unrealistic and unattainable ideals that essentially become a full-time job themselves.

I don't have time to live the life that many of those books suggest; few of us do.

I know these are excuses. What makes it worse is that I have many friends who make the necessary sacrifices to live past these excuses into difficult commitments for justice.

I applaud them. I admire them. I want to be more like them.

I confess that the ethics that drive my spending patterns and consumption are a tangle of contradictions, and I'm stumbling forward, trying to untangle them.

However, there are a few values that have guided my social consciousness as it relates to the ethics of consumption.

Living below your means

There are few obvious cultural marks of being an American, but one of them is living above one's means. This is an observation, not a judgment. It's not a judgment because the system in the United States allows for even moderately poor persons to borrow money to buy a house or a car or to pay for education.

I remember, during my freshman year of college, going to the university bookstore to buy the stack of required readings for my first-semester classes.

I was shocked by the total cost, and the bookstore clerk, obviously aware of the impact this had on incoming students, handed me a credit card application.

And that's how it begins for many people. Credit cards are the gateway drug of living above our means. This cultural dynamic becomes a kind of prison that convolutes and malforms our view of reality.

People sometimes refer to themselves as "poor college students" while accumulating tens of thousands of dollars of student loans—a considerable fortune for a large portion of the world's population.

What's ironic is that these average Americans who lament their disadvantaged state are actually among the world's richest five percent.

And this easy recourse to borrowing is also important, when you consider that lack of sustainable access to opportunity and resources is central to understanding poverty. The mere fact that we have access to credit, loans and debt cannot make us poor in the eyes of the world.

In most places on the face of the earth, people who can't afford to go to school don't get to go—they don't have the *luxury* of going into debt to pay for their school uniforms, books and tuition, or housing.

Living above one's means is not sustainable, let alone responsible; and it certainly doesn't reflect respect for friends who are poor.

Giving generously

Shortly after my wife and I married, we visited friends in Hong Kong. We knew they lived very simply and survived on missionary support, so we tried to pick up the tab everywhere we went. But they insisted on paying for everything.

77

Once after lunch, when the bill came, I asked whether they'd let us pay just that one time. They wouldn't. Our friends replied, "We're happy to get this for you. We've learned you can't out-give God."

That statement immediately became a truth we committed to live into. My wife and I began practicing that principle, not as a challenge or a test to see whether God would "repay" us for what we gave away, but as a statement of faith in God's goodness and God's desire that none should go without.

We still try to live into this posture of generous faithfulness. We know that we, ourselves, are in every way dependent on God's generous kindness.

Spending to celebrate

If you know people who are very, very poor, then you know that many of them are extremely generous. Some of the poorest friends I have are the most resourceful. Some of the most desperate people I know have the deepest faith.

What surprises me the most, though, is that those who live in some of the worst conditions always throw the best parties. In parts of South America, I've stayed up all night, eating and drinking more than I should have, celebrating a wedding or a birthday.

My friends who are desperately poor have taught me how to celebrate. They've taught me that one of the best things I can do with the access to resources given me is to spend them on someone else—spend them on celebrating the gift of friends, family and life.

When we reflect on the life of Christ, we often find him at the table, eating and drinking with friends. We frequently find Christ at parties, celebrating people.

In the world's great religions, the promises and metaphors of paradise are often imaged as a great banquet, suggesting that sharing meals at the table is an existential human experience that in some way is a practice for the afterlife.

Recovering responsibility

Finally, social responsibility has to inform how we spend.

What holds me accountable is relationships; friendships with people who are poor have become the prophetic presence of Christ in my life, reminding me to live a life that reflects respect for their condition.

If there's one thing I've learned, it's that our friends, our community and our faith have to help guide us in untangling the messy ethics of being a consumer.

We won't get it right. If we're American, we *will* leave a carbon footprint much larger than our neighbors from the Majority World. We honestly can't offset it.

But in authentic relationships with people who are poor, we can challenge the donor/receptor roles and follow them to God's heart. We can learn to be generous in new ways. We can make celebration a central part of our spirituality by finding the gifts and graces in life to honor. We can become imaginative, thoughtful and creative people who live simply for life's redemptive possibilities.

And we can recover responsibility by finding the courage to confess our shortcomings, stumbling forward, continuing to grapple with the issues.

This essay is used by permission of Christ Heurertz and was originally published on January 14, 2014, on *Faith & Leadership*, a blog offered by Duke Divinity School.

Christopher L. Heuertz fights for a renewal of contemplative activism and has spent his life bearing witness to the possibility of hope in a world that has legitimate reasons to question God's goodness. After graduating from college, Heuertz moved to India, where Mother Teresa mentored him for three years. There he helped launch South Asia's first pediatric AIDS care home. For 20 years, Heuertz served with Word Made Flesh working for women and children trafficked into the commercial sex industry.

Heuertz serves on the board of several nonprofits, and in 2012, he and his wife, Phileena, started Gravity: A Center for Contemplative Activism. He is the author of several books, including his most recent, Unexpected Gifts: Discovering the Way of Community. *On Twitter: @ChrisHeuertz.*

THURSDAY. Christmas Message 2013.
Rev. Dr. Naim Ateek

Christmas Message 2013

"In that region there were shepherds living in the fields, keeping watch over their flock by night" (Luke2:8).

"...after Jesus was born in Bethlehem of Judea, wise men from the East came to Jerusalem..." (Matthew 2:1).

The fact that the Christmas story mentions only two groups of visitors to the Christ child in Bethlehem, has, I believe, a theological significance. The shepherds in first century Palestine represented one of the lowest social strata in society. Religious tradition of Jesus' day labeled them as unclean. They were marginalized, poor, and considered as the scum of society; while the wise men represented the well to do, the educated, and the scholars of their day. The theological implication is clear: God's love for all people was expressed in and through the coming of Jesus Christ. This love welcomed both the shepherds and the wise men. True love does not differentiate between God's children. In Christ, the evil of discrimination and bigotry is obliterated.

Moreover, the shepherds were presumably Jewish, while the wise men were foreigners. Since the wise men came from "the East," a number of New Testament scholars have suggested that they came from Arabia. There is a further theological significance here. Both Jews and Arabs came to offer their homage to the Christ child. When we stand before God, not only do our social differences lose their importance, our racial differences are also eradicated. God's love for all people was being communicated regardless of social and financial status in society and regardless of racial background. Not only do rich and poor, Jew and Gentile stand before God as equals, there are also no political boundaries. All are welcomed and accepted. In other words, when we stand before the holy, our racism and bigotry should melt away, and we should become authentically human recognizing the other as a brother and a sister.

One of our most disturbing issues during this Christmas season is the situation of the shepherds and farmers of today, namely, the Bedouins of the Negev who are citizens of Israel. The Israeli government plans to Judaize the Negev by forcibly relocating tens of thousands of Bedouins from their ancestral lands on which most of them have lived for hundreds of years, long before the state of

Israel came into being. Israel wants to force them away from their lands and traditional way of life for the benefit of Israeli Jewish citizens. It is essentially a land grab. Many local and international human rights organizations have condemned Israel's actions and policies as discriminatory and in violation of international law.

During this Christmas season, Sabeel calls attention to the plight of the Bedouin community of the Negev that numbers between 160 to 200 thousand, and where thousands of them are living in villages that the government of Israel does not recognize. Consequently, Israel deprives them of basic services like education, electricity, running water, and sanitation.

This year's Christmas message emphasizes the fact that our faith demands of us to champion today's shepherds and farmers—the Bedouins—and advocate for their rights. The appalling irony is that what the Jewish people longed for over the centuries when they were weak, they are unwilling to give to others now that they have become strong. For hundreds of years, Jews wished and longed for human dignity, equality, and respect for their human rights, but tragically, the Israeli government today is unwilling to grant the same to its own citizens, the Bedouins of the Negev.

Christmas affirms God's love and concern for all human beings and especially to the most vulnerable, today's shepherds and farmers, the Bedouin community of the Negev.

......

On behalf of Sabeel's board and staff, I extend our best Christmas and New Year wishes to all our friends. I would like to seize this opportunity to thank all those friends who joined us at Sabeel's 9th international conference in Jerusalem last month when we addressed the theme of the "Bible and the Palestine-Israel conflict."

Naim Ateek

6 December 2013

The Rev. Dr. Naim Ateek is Director of the Sabeel Ecumenical Liberation Theology Center, Jerusalem. Sabeel works for justice, peace, and reconciliation in Palestine-Israel. Their website is www.sabeel.org.

FRIDAY. What if our Border Walls Keep out Mary and Baby Jesus? *Maryada Vallet*

She walks the dusty trails until her ankles swell and her back pulsates in pain. Her womb, distended in the eighth month of pregnancy, slows her down, yet also gives her an almost transcendent determination. With each step she is aware of her anxious thoughts, *Will I be left in the middle of nowhere to give birth among the rocks and thorny bushes? Does anyone out there care to take me in, give me shelter? What will the future hold for this special baby boy that I carry?*

Mary, the brave young woman who carried Jesus across borders trying to please the mandates of the Roman Empire most likely asked herself the same questions. Yet today "Mary" is not accompanied by a spouse and there definitely is no pleasing the empire. Instead of a donkey helping with her journey, she has a *coyote*, or people smuggler, who leaves her behind.

After two days of wandering alone in a strange desert land, desperately petitioning the Lord for help, someone does hear her cry, but instead of providing her with hospitality and protection, she is thrown into a cold detention center without medical attention, food, or water. She is told in no uncertain terms that at the United States border there is no room at the inn.

This "Mary" known as Maria pleads and cries as she is dumped back to the other side of a borderline, facing the violent and unknown streets in her vulnerable state. That's where, as a No More Deaths humanitarian volunteer, our lives intersected and my season of Advent became one of the most meaningful of my life. Maria asks me how it is possible that there is no room on the other side, when in comparison to the increasingly violent and poor place she comes from the land to the north seems so prosperous and abundant. Even more, she wonders how it can be that there is no room at this time when she has previously spent years laboring in U.S. factories and chicken slaughterhouses. The situation is even more complex as Maria thinks about her other children, two little boys—American citizens, waiting for her with anticipation and grief to return to their home in a Midwest city.

With every day that passes, Maria is closer to her due date, which could possibly be Christmas. She has no other choice but to give birth in a humble apartment provided by nuns, far from all family and friends. More than likely, the poor shepherds and neighbors of our time who hear the news will visit her and the new baby. This stable sits juxtaposed just blocks from the greatest power and wealth this world has known, surrounded by heavily enforced walls.

There are record high numbers of women and children, as well as tens of thousands of unaccompanied minors, coming to the US-Mexico border from neighboring countries to the south. Our country's leaders have called this situation a humanitarian crisis, but their response is to build more detention centers and implement more aggressive border enforcement to keep them out. But if Jesus lives among the orphan, widow and stranger, we very well may be keeping him out as well.

As we sing carols, look at lights and admire the miniature nativity scenes adorning our homes this holiday, let us not forget the most foundational elements of the Christmas story and how they come to life even today. All around us are strangers wandering the land looking for an open door and asking for compassion and justice—not detention, deportation and criminal status. May we not miss our chance to welcome and learn from them, as they have much to bring and to teach about the heart of our Lord. Indeed, they are the hope for our future that comes to us humble and expectant. Not unlike the baby Jesus.

Adapted from blog originally published at *Sojourners Magazine: www.sojo.net.*

Maryada Vallet, originally from Arizona, has kept busy as a border humanitarian, health professional, activist and evangelical agitator on the US-Mexico border since 2005. Most recently, Maryada has worked with World Vision International in humanitarian response projects, with her alma mater Azusa Pacific University as an adjunct professor, and as a consultant for international humanitarian organizations. For more on US-Mexico border humanitarian work and faith-based principles for immigration reform : www.nomoredeaths.org.

SATURDAY. *Gather, Feast, Create*

Gather

This week offers an opportunity to gather and contemplate our relationship to other cultures and traditions. Writers this week have shared thoughts about St. Lucy, Mary, Guadalupe (Mary), and simplicity. Before the meal, which should be quite festive, consider this contemplation offered on December 12 by Rev. Jessie Smith, an Episcopal priest in Washougal, Washington, at the end of her essay "A Letter to Mary." Dinner guests should bring with them a natural object or gather one before the meal:

I invite you into a few minutes of silence. Think about your own letter to Mary. Who is she to you? What hard, sharp edges do you need her to love?

During this time of silence I invite you to come forward and add your rock or whatever natural object you have with you, to the display [perhaps this becomes the table centerpiece.]

As you place your rock down join me in holding in mind a rough place, a sharp edge, a dangerous zone, a bleeding wound that could use some of Mary's mothering, strong, enduring, and nurturing love.

In remembrance of the many people who struggle financially during this time of year, consider as a group collecting gently used toys and taking them to a "Toys for Tots" bin or pooling money to purchase an item from an organization like Heifer International.

Feast

Meal: Southwestern foods potluck

The Feast of Guadalupe is truly a feast in Latin American countries and communities. While living in Texas, we enjoyed attending a big dinner party where tamales were served. Ideas for this meal could be enchiladas, tacos, nachos, sangria, or any of your favorite Latin dishes. Tamales may often be purchased from freezer sections in grocery stores or from families who make large batches to sell for extra income during this time of the year.

Create

Another tradition enjoyed in many Latin communities is the *las posadas* procession and celebration. *Posada* means "dwelling" in Spanish. In this drama, actors portray the roles of Joseph and Mary, the innkeeper, and others in the nativity scene. On each of nine nights, the procession walks around the village square while "Mary" and "Joseph" knock on doors and ask for a room. At the end of the procession, they are welcomed in to either a church or a home where a feast and party await. Children often get to try and knock down a piñata and scramble for the candy. Read more on www.worldofchristmas.net. Enacting this drama as a group would be a fun, tangible way to relate to this story.

—Kristin

O EMMANUEL

"O Emmanuel, king and lawgiver, desire of the nations, Savior of all people, come and set us free, Lord our God."

Week Three of Advent

[Image: Manhattan]

O God-with-Us

"Emmanuel." The name rolls smoothly off the tongue, sounds exotic to English-speaking ears. We sing the mysterious name throughout this season. The tune to "O Come, O Come Emmanuel" is plaintive, full of longing. In the verse we probably know best, we ask Emmanuel to "ransom captive Israel/that mourns in lowly exile here/until the Son of God appears." Why are we Gen X and Gen Y, Millenials, and Baby Boomers chanting these verses year after year? Perhaps mostly out of tradition, but maybe also from the comfort these verses offer that more closely meets our emotions around this time in Advent, when we are a bit frazzled from all of the lists and obligations, tired of hoping our children don't grow up to be planet-trashing selfish consumers because they don't "get" the "'true' meaning of Christmas," a little more than worried about how the in-laws will get along or how we will pay the credit card bill. We may feel weary and isolated even in the midst of all of the "holiday cheer" around us, the vibrant colors, flashing lights, ecstatic "Christmas carols" demanding we play our parts, whether we are at the gas station pumping fuel as "Holly Jolly Christmas" bombards us or waiting in line at the Post Office to ship parcels while "Walkin' in a Winter Wonderland" makes us wish we were.

In the midst of that, maybe we slow down and relax when we hear those minor melancholy chords of "O Come, O Come Emmanuel." We feel exiled. We find hope when we remember the Israelites. We feel a kinship to the Hebrew captives, longing for a homeland, for a Messiah. They got Moses—then longed for more—since their deeper bondage wasn't to Pharaoh, but within their spiritual selves. So, they cried out to God and God answered: Emmanuel, "God With Us." In the hymn, the writer is referring to Isaiah 7:14, "Behold, a virgin shall conceive, and bear a son, and shall call His name Immanuel."

God came to be with us, and God still comes to be with us. He was born to Mary, a name that still evokes all sorts of reactions and emotions: confusion, endearment, courage, anger even. Her story is timeless and challenging. We scratch our heads over the idea of a "virgin birth" and piety. We wonder why some Christians honor her more—or less—than we do; even appear to worship her, or ignore her. And what about her relationship with Joseph—and whatever happened to him?

Several of this week's reflections are focused on Mary and also on the blessing and wisdom and hope that may be found by welcoming in unexpected visitors and situations in our midst. As we imagine traveling the road to Bethlehem with the Holy Family and arriving at the Biblical manger scene, who can we invite along? Who is Mary to us? And how do we need her Emmanuel to come and be with us this week?

—Kristin

Prayer for Week Three of Advent

Come home to God, Emmanuel,
the One who lives with us,
eternally enlivening, eternally guiding.

Come home to God.
Let the remembrance of Jesus' birth
captivate your heart
and fill you with a longing for more.

Come home to God.
Let the coming of the living God
grab your attention.
Set aside what does not matter.
Remember the things that do.

Come home to God.
Unclutter your life.
Take time to notice God's presence.
Let it flood your heart.
Let it drench your soul.
Let it overflow your spirit.

Come home to God.
Desire nothing else.
Strive with every breath
for the coming of God's eternal world,
with its promise of wholeness
for all creation.

Come, Lord Jesus, welcome us home.

—Christine

SUNDAY. A Combat Veteran at the Manger. *David W. Peters*

You almost don't see him slip in the stable door. He enters the stable cautiously, but quickly. He sees who is inside and what they're holding in their hands. He feels OK and takes another step in. The first thing he does is walk around the manger to the stone wall on the back side of the stable. He does this because he's a combat veteran, and he always does this. One time, he didn't, and the memory of his failure haunts him. Evans died that day. Evans was a young kid, right out of high school. The veteran wasn't much older, but he was responsible for his life, and his death. Evans took the first round in the chest, in his body armor. The second, he took in his windpipe. He couldn't even cry out for his mother.

The veteran sees Evan's face in every young face, but especially in the face of young Joseph, the guy who just became a father. The veteran remembers becoming a father. Both his son and his daughter were born when he was overseas. His son was born during his first combat tour in Iraq, and his daughter during his second tour in Afghanistan—or was it the other way around. His lieutenant joked at the time that soldiers only need to be there for the conception.

He saw his kids when he came home. After a few days, they knew him. Now, as he looks at the baby in the manger, he can see the vulnerability of this little one and all the little ones that are born during war. He hopes his own kids know him to be more than just a soldier who is never there. He hopes they know that he's a good guy, even though he shot and killed two men during the last time he was in Iraq. The veteran hopes the baby in the manger knows this, too.

The veteran is not an old man, but he thinks like one. The word veteran means "old" in Latin, after all. He hopes that his babies, and this baby, can make the world a better place. He hopes his babies, and this baby, don't have to suffer and die in a war. He hopes these things, but he knows too much about the cruel side of the world to imagine a world without the careless atrocities of war. Every time he sees a baby, he hopes this.

The veteran grew up in a church where the preachers told him that God was good and that God loved the world. Somewhere, when he held Evans as he gurgled for breath, he stopped believing God cared about anything that happened on this planet. If God cared, he reasoned, then he would do

91

something to stop some of the cruelty and violence in the world. God didn't stop any of it, especially the violence that the veteran had to visit upon his enemies.

A tear forms in his eyes and he chokes it back, trying not to cry about the death and destruction he has seen, and still sees, in the darkness of his mind.

Around thirty years later, another veteran, a Roman Centurion, a Sergeant Major, stands on a hillside called "The Place of the Skull." He is the one who says of this baby, "Truly, this man was the Son of God" (Mark 15:39).

The evangelist in Mark's gospel is a combat veteran. He bears witness to the good news for planet earth that is found in the baby in the manger.

In World War I, the Episcopal Church issued a Service Cross to all the men who volunteered to fight in Europe. Military chaplains and local parishes still give them out to warriors today. On the front of the cross are the words, "Christ Died for You." Jesus' death is for everyone, without exception and without distinction. That is why we can all gather around his manger on this silent, holy night.

David W. Peters served as an enlisted Marine and Army chaplain in Iraq. He is the author of Death Letter: God, Sex, and War, *and a contributor to the* Huffington Post. *David lives with his wife, Sarah, in Austin, Texas.*

MONDAY. Too Old and Decrepit to Bless? *Anne Townsend*

There are times when the very old may become like children to some of us. We bathe, feed, cuddle and play with them, change their nappies, clear up their messes, dress them and push them around in pushchairs.

But, in their helplessness and dependency, like small children, they may be an unexpected source of blessing. I discovered this on the roadside grass verge, by the A3 Tibbett's Corner roundabout, where my 100-year old mother and I were enjoying our weekly cup of tea and sticky bun from Jake's Burger Bar. She had had a severe stroke seven years earlier, was paralysed, couldn't speak, and lived in her wheelchair.

It was an ordinary kind of a morning. Ordinary things were going on around us. The workmen munched their bacon butties [24] as usual, the buses and vans swerved round the corners, the sun shone feebly. They chatted to my mother, ignoring the fact that although her eyes indicated that she understood, like a preverbal child, she could not audibly reply to them.

Then I noticed the man in his late sixties moving slowly across the grass, his eyes fixed on the ground, as if searching for hidden treasure. But it wasn't treasure he was after. His job was to notice and pick up every piece of litter scattered on the ground. He was doing this intently, as if his life depended on it.

Our eyes met and we exchanged smiles. "Morning!" we said to each other. His ebony face was furrowed, his eyes sad, and I wondered what had brought him to England from the other side of the world. He looked more like a teacher or doctor than refuse collector. Was he doing this work because this was the best he could find to help to support growing grandchildren?

By the time my mother and I were ready to return to her Care Home, he'd disappeared. I carefully pushed her wheelchair along the pavement, and noticed him a little way ahead. We caught up. I nodded in the direction of my mother commenting: "She's over 100 years old!"

Pleasure and respect swept across his face. He drew closer, stuttering in broken English: "In my country, we'd ask someone this old to give us a blessing." I realised that my mother understood and was nodding to me. "Would you like

---

[24] Editor's note: "bacon butties" is English slang for bacon sandwiches.

her to do this for you?" His face lit up, and he knelt in front of her on the pavement.

I gently placed her paralyzed hand on his head, and uttered the words I knew she'd want to say herself had she been able to: "May God's blessing rest on you and yours, now and forever. Amen."

Three pairs of eyes filled with tears as we parted. My mother was still able to serve God by the quality of life she lived in the Care Home and even at Jake's Burger Bar despite severe disability and suffering.

Anne lives in Bromley, UK. She worked as a missionary doctor with the Overseas Missionary Fellowship in Thailand for 16 years. On return to the UK, she worked as editor of Christian Family Magazine, *and then as National Director of CARE Trust. Following a transforming breakdown and crisis of faith, she trained as a psychoanalytic psychotherapist and worked with clergy and religious facing emotional and spiritual difficulties. She was in the first wave of women to be ordained as priests in the Church of England, has written a number of books including:* Faith Without Pretending, Good Enough for God, *and,* Hidden Treasure. *She has three adult children, six grandchildren, and a husband with early Alzheimer's.*

TUESDAY. This Will Be A Sign For You.
David Perry

In the centre of town, fenced off in a demolition site awaiting redevelopment, the sole surviving interior wall of a once private washroom is now open to the elements. Set above the rotting surround for a pair of long-removed hand washbasins, two mirrors reflect the immediate surroundings. Their surfaces bear the marks of violence, exhibiting the telltale signs of impact damage. This could have occurred as the building was being demolished, or it might bear testimony to rocks, bricks or stones thrown by vandals at such an easy and tempting target afterwards.

Like razor-sharp spider webs, spun within the structure of the glass, the crazed and splintered patterns look like their sole purpose is to capture meaning and prevent it escaping from the mirrored surface intact. Such violence has achieved its aim: the picture is disjointed, broken, distorted, difficult to interpret or see as a unified and intelligible whole. The shattered mirrors convey the truth of the world's brokenness and suffering. Everywhere violence inhibits us from seeing the picture of a world perfectly reflecting the love of God. Violence breaks up the image, smashes it into sharp-edged pieces which hurt and harm. Violence splinters meaning and traps our perception into falsely chaotic and hope-denying mindsets.

Across the world the mirror of everyday experience is shattered daily by violence. The brutality of dictators and the mindless, murderous impulses of disaffected young men take the lives of the innocent, especially women and children. Domestic violence and abuse, hidden away in every community, wreaks havoc in a similarly destructive way with clenched fists and brutalizing words. All around us mirrors of expectation and promise are shattered and smashed; cruelly, deliberately and vengefully.

Violence would smash and destroy all possibility of us seeing God's reflection in the image of contemporary life. The Bible knows differently. If the perfect picture of God's loving Kingdom is broken into myriads of apparently faith denying shards, our Christian faith tells us that it is within the splintered, broken picture that we should expect to discover God alongside us, amongst us, reaching out to us. God never abandons us. Within the shattered heart of life, God remains lovingly faithful and true: the ancient promises hold good and God is always and utterly merciful. Mary knew this and claimed it for herself and her son: **"in remembrance of his mercy, according to the promise he made"** (Luke 1:54-55, New Revised Standard Version). The life of Jesus was God's incarnate gift of self within the very splinters and shards of human experience.

The sign of this truth is that God is with us and we should expect to encounter that reality for ourselves: **"to you is born this day in the city of David a Saviour, who is the Messiah, the Lord. This will be a sign for you: you will find a child wrapped in bands of cloth and lying in a manger"** (Luke 2:11-12, NRSV). Looking into the mirrors, we can see a face, a woman's face, reflected in one of the broken pieces of glass. She is looking at us. And we realise that she must be standing close by. In the second photograph this splintered truth is picked out in colour.[25] Mary stood in the brokenness of her time and place and Jesus was born right there where the splintered patterns of poverty, death and violence were at their worst.

---

[25] For the color version of David Perry's second photograph, please see the original *Godspace* blog posted on December 20, 2012.

We see Mary on God's side of the image. She allows us to perceive a different reality all around us, one that violence cannot deny or obliterate. The *Magnificat* puts this picture into words. In his birth, Jesus is the very disclosure of this divine presence and purpose which confronts and confounds violence. Today, as at that first Christmas, God looks out at us with love from within all the razor-sharp shards of horror that would deny God's very existence. This will be a sign for you; a sign to turn around and see the God-picture which challenges the distorted brokenness of our human behaviour and perception.

Cracked mirror with shard showing woman's face—Dave Perry

Dave is a Methodist Minister who blogs at www.visualtheology.blogspot.com. *A passionate photographer, he is keen to use visual imagery as a way of bringing the faith alive. He has recently published two new books,* Quandary *and* looking up looking around looking closely. *Dave is currently Superintendent of the Hull (Centre and West) Circuits in East Yorkshire in the U.K.*

And Mary said,

"My soul magnifies the Lord,
and my spirit rejoices in God my Savior,
for he has looked on the humble estate of his servant.
For behold, from now on all generations will call me blessed;
for he who is mighty has done great things for me,
and holy is his name.
And his mercy is for those who fear him
from generation to generation.
He has shown strength with his arm;
he has scattered the proud in the thoughts of their hearts;
he has brought down the mighty from their thrones
and exalted those of humble estate;
he has filled the hungry with good things,
and the rich he has sent away empty.
He has helped his servant Israel,
in remembrance of his mercy,
as he spoke to our fathers,
to Abraham and to his offspring forever."

(Luke 1:46-55, English Standard Version)

WEDNESDAY. Virgin Mary and the Bible's Answer to Human Trafficking.
Rev. Rajkumar Boaz Johnson

The New Testament[26] has many examples regarding the restoration of women to a place of honor. The narrative of the life of Jesus in Matthew poignantly begins with underlining the lives of five women: Tamar (Gen. 38); Rahab (Josh. 2); Ruth, wife of Uriah (2 Sam. 11, 12); and Mary. Four of these women were sexually abused and trafficked by men in positions of power and authority. In spite of the horrible life faced by these women, the Bible elevates them to the highest status; they become the bearers of the Messiah seed. In doing so, paradigmatically, the Bible is elevating the status and name of all women who are abused and trafficked as a result of systemic evil in human history. The fifth woman, Mary, also grew up among girls who were regularly abused and trafficked by the Sadducees and the Roman soldiers. This was the reason that the most common name given to girls was Miriam, meaning "bitter," since the life of the girl was assumed to be full of bitterness due to sexual abuse and human trafficking. Yet, miraculously, one girl was preserved, a virgin, to bear the Messiah of the world! She was not a virgin because she was the only one who was pure. She was a virgin because of a miraculous preservation of one girl. Mary becomes, in many senses, a symbol of hope for all girls throughout history, all over the world, who are trafficked and abused by fallen humanity. This is indeed a thick answer to the problem of human trafficking.

The Messiah born by Mary elevated the status of so many women that he encountered. He knew what his own mother had gone through. She was ostracized by the so-called high-class people, for carrying and bearing a child out of wedlock. He himself was called a *mamzer*—a term reserved for the children born by women who were sexually abused by Roman soldiers. During his public ministry, Jesus, knowing the horrible life faced by women around him, always reached out to them and restored their dignity. A good example is Jesus' encounter with the Samaritan woman at the well in John 4. Jesus knew that Samaritan women were abused on a far more regular basis than low-class

---

[26]Note from Christine Sine: We tend to think of Mary's pregnancy as a joyful time of celebration. Today's essay about human trafficking during the times that Mary grew up, helps us to understand some of the challenges she would have faced even before Christ was conceived.

Jewish women. They were the lowest of the low people group in the society around Jesus. They were constantly and systematically abused, just because they were Samaritans. During his conversation with her, at a poignant moment, Jesus asks her to "Go call your man." She shrugs her shoulders and says, "I have no man." Jesus says to her, "I know what you have gone through. I know that you really have had no man. Each of the other five have sexually abused you and battered you. The person who has you now is not really your man" (John 4:17-18, paraphrased). To this woman who had suffered so much because of systemic evil against women, Jesus offered the water of life—the water which alone could heal her deepest wounds. The rest of the narrative is a powerful example of how Jesus heals and elevates the status of a trafficked woman. She goes back to her town, and the whole village listens to her words. This woman, who was trafficking material and was sexually abused by men around her, is suddenly transformed into an *eshet chayil*, a strong woman.

The whole Bible has one narrative after another of the transformation of the status of women in society. It begins with a very strong place for the woman. She is no ordinary helper to man. She is a divinely placed savior figure—*ezer kenegdo*. Rather sadly, throughout history, human beings have destroyed and desecrated women. Evil men have shattered their true identity as strong help while women have been sexually abused and trafficked. Yet, in powerful ways, the Bible recreates the identity and the place of women. The Bible restores women to their creation identity of being *eshet chayil*—emotionally, physically, spiritually, and mentally strong women. They were created to be savior figures for humanity. This is the strongest and thickest answer to the problem of human trafficking.

This article was originally published as part of the series The Bible's Answer to Human Trafficking *in* Christians for Biblical Equality's *weekly ezine* arise. *The articles were written by Rev. Rajkumar Boaz Johnson (PhD, Trinity International University and Trinity Evangelical Divinity School) a professor of Biblical and Theological Studies at North Park University in Chicago, IL. This is the third and final article of the series on human trafficking. For links to Parts 1 and 2 of the series, please visit:*
http://www.cbeinternational.org/resources/bibles-answer-human-trafficking-part-3.

THURSDAY. Wading Through Hot Chocolate and Cloudy Skies.
Kim Balke

Hurting people billow about me,

darkening grays, aging ways,

black and purple-blue hues;

a hollowed out sky before me

in the form of needs, misdeeds,

unkempt, messy vapours diffusing light and telltale sight

around my landscape. Let them go, too heavy to hold.

Falling, falling inevitably down over autumn leaves

in a colour leeching rain; a desired disintegration into ground,

the still, waiting space and time for growing something good…later.

Here and now is damp and cold;

a stick stirring a muck of memories,

a jump in puddles day;

watch the slough carry leaf boats downstream and away,

far away to adventure lands;

catch my breath and here I go

into William Blake's "eternity in an hour"

flowers, unfolding long-forgotten freckle-faced smiles

of an incognito princess ship wrecked on new shores;

in the dirt on her tattered sleeves, the gifts of Magi sustain her;

in the wet socks hanging to dry, shepherds guard flocks at night.

She is waiting for…no…

she is wading through hot chocolate!

Her face peers into steam, Anna-like, searching through temple crowds,
 wondering.

She finds herself enveloped in rainbow, gloria and God given promises

from an ancient red and black letter book

about a baby-king wrapped in rags, hand-me-down clothes

from prophets to Elizabeth to Mary;

stitched and mended Metaphor of Meaning

for the fullness of time;

for child's play in the sacredness of this present pregnant moment

seen in cloudy Tsawwassen skies and me.

Kim Balke has been a leaf chaser and cloud wanderer since early childhood. She grew up in southern Ontario near the Great Lakes with family roots in Nova Scotia, where she has been a beachcomber for mermaid's tears (beach glass, especially the blue ones) for over ten years. She now lives on the West Coast in a small community, Tsawwassen, BC, surrounded by ocean and river mystery. She is married to Tom, fellow wanderer in creation, and has two young adult sons, one dog and a huge family of stick bugs. She is an Expressive Arts Therapist in private practice and work with children in three schools in the Lower Mainland of Vancouver, British Columbia.

FRIDAY. Coming Home: The Story God is Giving me through Infertility.
Andrea Frankenfeld

I know Advent isn't about Christmas trees or baking cookies in the shape of a candy cane.

It's about the tradition, or discipline, of waiting. We wait because we believe it is worth it. We wait because we know God is faithful. We know he is our reward—no matter our circumstances.

Like most people, I hate waiting, but I can't deny God has used the pain of waiting to turn my heart toward him. When my husband and I started thinking about having children, we expected that it would happen like it does for everyone.

We expected that when we were ready, we would start our family, renewing the years with younger versions of ourselves.

It never crossed my mind that becoming a mother wasn't certain, but in fact a fragile hope, no more and no less than a prayer submitted to a sovereign God.

Many years have passed with nothing to show for my prayer, save some grief, an ever-intense longing and God's nearness.

My story isn't extremely unique. As I read through Abraham's story in Genesis, I see the story of broken humanity transformed by God's faithfulness, a foreshadowing of the Jesus who would come to redeem us in spite of our sinfulness.

In our early years of longing for children, my husband and I followed the Lord to India on mission. We sacrificed many things to fulfill this calling. When we, eventually, returned home to the U.S., we had no clear direction and were no closer to being parents.

I knew God was good and powerful because I had seen him work in my life before. I wrestled with God. There were — and still are — dark moments.

Despite my trust in God's faithfulness, I long for a different story.

The story of infertility is not one I would have chosen for myself, but it is the one God is giving me.

For me, coming home is about acknowledging the home I have in relationship with Christ — with or without children.

Because our home is not made up of children, I am tempted to think no one is impacted by my traditions.

But, my heart is changing while I wait. Becoming more like Jesus doesn't mean forsaking or burying my human pieces. It means redeeming them. Yielding them. Learning to be unapologetically broken. Letting him replace my broken pieces with wholeness. Realizing that the deepest longing I have can only be met in Christ.

When my home is an authentic place where people are welcome, I'm choosing to be proud of my story.

In a season when everyone is busy, I can focus on simple things that reflect what home means to me. A cozy house with space for a few more at our table. Time to listen and share life with a friend. Abundant blessings to share with others. Quiet evenings to savor with my husband.

Over the last five years, I've decorated two artificial Christmas trees in two states and two countries. I've sung Christmas carols in the homes of Indian people who don't know about Jesus. I've celebrated warm-weather Christmas mornings with my Indian family at the early dawn. I've played more games of Dirty Santa than I can count in Bible Belt America. I've hosted large and small numbers of people in my home.

I've slowed down to notice the people around me, the people God has put in front of me. I've considered my place as my mission field — whether it's in the Southern Bible Belt, the progressive Pacific Northwest or urban India.

I continue to wait for a child until God leads my heart in another direction, but I still want to know when the waiting will end. I want to make the longing go away.

But the season of Advent reminds me that it never will. It's worth waiting to know more of Jesus.

Because we don't have children, I get to be more creative about how to include people in my traditions. I just have to be willing to live out my story and be intentional enough to gather others around.

Because I belong to Jesus, I always have a home. In my home, there is hope that transcends my circumstances. I can wait in either grief or joy.

And, I will wait. Hope is coming.

Andrea Frankenfeld is a writer, editor and consultant who lives in the Seattle area with her husband. Despite her Southern roots and missionary heart, Andrea feels at home in the beauty of the Pacific Northwest. Some of her favorite things are traveling to new places, sharing tea with new and old friends and analyzing movies with her husband. She blogs regularly at http://www.coffeeandcondensation.com/ *and* http://www.andreafrankenfeld.com/.

SATURDAY. *Gather, Feast, Create*

Gather

The twelve days of Christmas are getting close! As you gather this week, discuss your plans for celebrating that season. Get out calendars and be intentional about setting aside time for activities that incarnate the themes of Christmas for you, your family, or community. Ideas to consider are:

• Spread out gift-giving over the twelve days of Christmas. Our family chooses different days to open gifts from packages we receive from friends and family who live far away. When children are young, this allows the opportunity to discuss who each gift giver is, instead of getting lost in stacks of presents under the Christmas tree.

• Share meals with neighbors you would like to know better or someone you would rather exclude from your table.

• Walk a labyrinth on New Year's Eve.

• Get creative with your nativity scene: place baby Jesus in the stable early on Christmas morning, before your household awakes; let the Magi spend all twelve days traveling from one room to another before reaching the holy family.

• Study Christmas traditions in different cultures and try cuisines from those countries.

• Donate toys to a children's charity on Holy Innocents Day (December 28).

- Go on a silent walk in nature on December 25, after gift opening and breakfast.

Feast

Meal: Potluck of favorite family recipes

This week, prepare a favorite family recipe and share stories about memories formed while eating that cuisine in the past, or if no favorites come to mind, begin a new tradition by sharing your favorite dish to cook.

Create

Consider writing a poem or prose reflection about your experience of Advent so far this year. Share with the group, if you choose. Alternately, those gathered might commit to a photo challenge for the twelve days of Christmas and share photographs taken each of the twelve days via social media or Email.

—Kristin

O CLAVIS DAVID

"O Key of David, O royal Power of Israel controlling at your will the gate of Heaven: Come, break down the prison walls of death for those who dwell in darkness and the shadow of death; and lead your captive people into freedom."

Week Four of Advent

[Image: Hallway at the now-decommissioned Eastern State Penitentiary]

O Key of David

Christmas is almost upon us, and our longing for the coming of the One who will break down all barriers and draw all creation into the love of God is almost unbearable. The great O Antiphon we have used to introduce this week speaks of this longing. In *A Monastery Journey to Christmas*, Brother Victor-Antoine D'Avila-Latourrette says:

> *Christ, the Messiah, the Key of David, comes to unlock for all, Jews and gentiles alike, the doors of the kingdom of God. He alone possesses the keys and it will be he who invites all, be they just or sinners, into his eternal banquet. No one shall be excluded. This is precisely the good news of the Gospel he will proclaim one day.*[27]

Brother Victor calls Jesus "the Prince of Peace whose face the whole world longs to see." And I would add "longs to come home to." I think that in the hearts of all humankind there is a deep ache for the coming of a saviour who will lead us home together. That desire, that longing to see the authentic face of God and to come home to a community into which all the peoples of the world are invited is very close as we move through these last few days of Advent.

As I look out at my seemingly dead Seattle garden, covered in frost and snow, I can fully appreciate this image. Winter seems to have destroyed all life, yet hidden in the earth, the roots still live, growing stronger, reaching deeper, ready to emerge in the coming spring. For the Jewish people, there was a long winter of centuries before Jesse's Root sprouted forth with the coming of Christ, the Messiah.

When Christ first appears, he is like the first sprouts of spring growth—weak, vulnerable, tiny compared to the tree that will grow. This is the Christ whose remembrance we celebrate at Christmas. Yet in that tiny shoot is the hope and promise of what is to come—a tree that will spread over all the earth, a saviour for the whole world whose power and scope is far greater than any of us could ever imagine. This is the Christ for whose coming we wait with joyful anticipation. This is the Christ who fills our hearts with longing for the future.

This tender shoot, this vulnerable child whose very birth reveals the upside down nature of God's kingdom is an ensign for the nations, a flag towards which all people will be drawn. The word we translate as "nations" had a very different meaning for the Jews. "Gentiles" were everyone who was not Jewish. It encompassed all peoples outside Israel, opening God's promise of salvation to all cultures and countries. The new kingdom Christ ushered in is open to the

---

[27] Brother Victor-Antoine D'Avila-Latourrette, *A Monastery Journey To Christmas* (Liguori: Liguori Publications, 2011), 114.

entire world. Christ the Messiah, the tiny Branch which will become a mighty tree, will break down walls and barriers between all people.

A Prayer for Christmas Eve.

Make room.
Let Christ be born
in the quiet and the innermost spaces
of your hearts.

Make room.
Let Christ be born
in the streets and in the ghettos,
in the famines and the plagues and in the wars.

Make room.
Let Christ be born
not far away in distant ages,
but in every heart and place
where love and faith are found.

Let Christ be born,
and find in us his Bethlehem.

—Christine

SUNDAY. mobile homes (not that kind).
Kathy Escobar

Growing up, I lived with a prevailing feeling I like to call "never being comfortable in my own skin or my own home." My mom was a single mom, doing the best she could, despite the obstacles. My dad, a sweet and kind man but a severe alcoholic, always lived in another state from us, renting rooms from people or living in a camper.

When I was in late elementary school I inherited a stepfather who had a positive (a stable job, so we owned a house for the first time) and a lot of negatives (he, too, drank a lot, but definitely wasn't sweet and kind). My role in the family was to be the glue that kept everything together. Keep the peace, be good, do good—this was my coping mechanism.

The problem was that inside, I was sort of falling apart. I wanted someone to be glue for me.

I wanted to feel comfortable in my skin.

I wanted to feel "at home" in my house.

I wanted to feel "at home" in my heart.

After graduating from high school, I left for college in another state, my car packed to the brim with most of my belongings. My mom ended up finally separating from my stepdad and selling the only house I remembered living in.

Looking back, I realize now I had already been homeless, even before the house was gone. Spiritually and emotionally homeless.

After college, I got married and started seeking God in more intentional ways. I also began to address some of the issues from my past. Really, most of them lead to that feeling of being emotionally homeless, displaced, lonely, never secure. Since then God has continued to do all kinds of crazy things in my life to bring healing and life into these dark places of my story. **As I continue to heal, I feel more and more at home in my own skin**. And, I have worked to create a home for my family and friends that is safe and loving for those who enter.

Over the years, it seems like my eyes keep being opened to this reality:

There are a lot of "homeless" people who live in houses. Men and women of all shapes, sizes, experiences, educations, faith backgrounds, ages, and colors who feel spiritually and emotionally homeless. Displaced. Disconnected. Unloved. With no sense of belonging or safety.

Some have been in churches for years, but have never felt the deep and meaningful connection with other people and God they long for. Others have never felt safe in a church for all kinds of reasons. **Whatever the reason, feeling "home" has eluded.**

When Jesus entered the world as a little baby, he had "no place to lay his head." Then, when he left home and entered public ministry, it was the same. However, his life was filled with friends, relationships, interactions with crazy people, weird parties, and a deep, passionate, intimate connection with God, the Father.

He was home, without a home.

Because He *was* a home.

A mobile home. A person who created a sense of safety and belonging and healing for those around Him, wherever He went.

Jesus left us with his example. I think that's what the incarnation of Christ is supposed to be—we are called to be mobile homes, people who create a sense of safety and love and hope in the places we go.

We don't have to be fully healed to create it. We don't have to have all of our ducks in a row or our Scripture verses properly memorized. We don't have to meet some magical bar in the sky that says what qualifies us.

The main thing we really need is a willingness to be present. (And maybe that is the hardest thing to give. I know it is for me.)

There is a whole desperate world out there, right in our own backyards. A world—no matter how rich or poor our neighborhoods might be—that is homeless and yearning for "home."

I think "home" can be created in ways that have nothing to do with four walls and a roof in a specific part of town.

Home is our hearts being connected to each other in a tangible way.

Home is a relationship that restores dignity, beauty, value where there once was none.

114

Home is a shared meal and a meaningful conversation about God and life that stirs the soul.

Home is the safety of showing the reality of the brokenness in our lives and having people not ditch us.

Home is a shared experience that makes us think.

Home is a desperate hug reciprocated.

Home is a group of people "where everybody knows your name and everybody's glad you came."

Home is the weird crazy sense that God is with us and will never leave us, no matter how dark it gets.

My hope on this downward path of living out the wild ways of Jesus is that in each of our own unique ways, we would become these kinds of mobile homes.

People sent out in a broken and disconnected world to somehow create a strange and beautiful sense of belonging wherever we go. People of hope. People of love. People of presence. People who are beginning to feel more at home in our own skin and can help others feel more "home," too.

This essay is reprinted with permission by Kathy Escobar. It originally appeared in *sheloves* magazine and then on December 17, 2013, at *kathyescobar.com* and *Godspace.*

Kathy is copastor of the Refuge, an eclectic beautiful faith community in north Denver, and juggles five kids & an awesome husband who has a bunch of jobs, too. She's an advocate for friends in hard places, a trained spiritual director, and loves to teach and facilitate events, workshops, and groups. She writes a little, hangs out with people a lot, and teaches college classes online because missional living doesn't pay the bills. These all blend together and make for one messy life in the trenches with people. Her newest book (Oct. 2014) is Faith Shift: Finding Your Way Forward When Everything You Believe is Coming Apart. *More of her work may be found at* www.kathyescobar.com.

MONDAY. Always Winter and Never Christmas. *Travis Mamone*

Around this time every year, I feel strangely melancholy. Like Charlie Brown, I know I should be happy; Christmas is coming, remember? While I am glad I can finally listen to *A Very Special Christmas Vol. 1* over and over again, I still have this underlying feeling of gloom.

Maybe it's the weather. After all, it is that time again to put away the flip-flops and T-shirts, and break out the heavy coats and sweaters. Plus, the days are getting shorter, so when I get off work it looks like the middle of night outside.

But I think it's something much deeper than that.

Call me a party pooper, but I can't help but think about all the people that won't have themselves a merry little Christmas. I think of the homeless man trying to keep warm, the little girl wondering why her poverty-stricken parents say they're not going to have a Christmas this year, and the lonely man who is thinking about ending his own life. I also think about my own life and all of the mistakes I've made during the past year, and all of the unresolved issues that are waiting for me in the new year. Maybe I am the Charlie Browniest of all the Charlie Browns in the world after all.

It's no wonder that one of my favorite Christmas songs is "Sister Winter" by Sufjan Stevens, one of the saddest Christmas songs ever. Most Christmas songs are about simply having a wonderful Christmastime. However, if you struggle with mental illness like I do, you know that the dark and cold winter can make you sad. Instead of thinking about all the good times you're going to have with your loved ones, you can't help but cry from all the pain you've experienced in the past year. December doesn't just mean Christmas and New Year's Eve; it also means having one last good cry before the year ends. And I think this song sums it up perfectly:

Oh my friends I've
Begun to worry right
Where I should be grateful
I should be satisfied

Oh my heart I
Would clap and dance in place

With my friends I have so
Much pleasure to embrace
But my heart is
Returned to sister winter
But my heart is
As cold as ice[28]

Or maybe it's all just part of the Advent season.

As we light [candles on] the Advent wreath and sing "O Come, O Come Emmanuel," we think about how this world, this life, isn't how God originally intended it to be. We think about the Second Advent, when all will be made new again, by meditating on the First. We pray for God to give us grace "that we may cast away works of darkness, and put upon us the armor of light"[29] as we prepare ourselves for the coming of Jesus.

Advent reminds me of *The Lion, the Witch, and the Wardrobe*, where it was "always winter and never Christmas"[30] in Narnia before Aslan came. I know it sounds like the title of a bad emo song, but once you think about it, this world does seem like it's in a state of always winter and never Christmas. We see so much darkness every time we watch the news: war, poverty, crime, corruption, hatred, etc. It seems like we'll never see the light; we only catch a few glimpses of the occasional flicker.

So maybe all of this melancholy is just my spirit groaning with creation to see the world restored (Romans 8:22-23). Maybe on a deeper level, I know that this isn't the best we can do. Maybe the reason why I haven't given up yet is because I know, deep within my heart, that another world is possible.

And one day we will see another world. One day, Christmas will come, and then the snow will melt away. One day will see, as Brian McLaren writes it, "the beginning of a new spiritual-historical age or era."[31]

But first, we must wait. It's only when we experience Advent—the season of waiting and preparation—that we can experience Christmas.

---

[28] Sufjan Stevens, *Sister Winter*, 2006 by Asthmatic Kitty Records. mp3.
[29] *The Book of Common Prayer* (Church Publishing Incorporated, 1979), 159.
[30] C.S. Lewis, *The Lion, the Witch, and the Wardrobe* (New York: HarperCollins Publishers, 1950), 19.
[31] Brian McLaren, *A New Kind of Christianity: Ten Questions That Are Transforming the Faith* (New York: HarperCollins Publishers, 2010), 197.

Travis is an author, a blogger, and an all-around wayfaring stranger. He is the author of the e-books In Praise of the Doubting Thomas, *and* O Come Emmanuel. *He has written for such publications as* Provoketive Magazine, Relevant Magazine, The Upper Room, *and* Burnside Writers Collective. *His work appears in the books* Not Alone: Stories of Living with Depression *(Civitas Press, 2011) and* Finding Church *(Civitas Press, 2012). He has also contributed to the* Something Beautiful *podcast. He lives in Easton, Maryland and blogs at* http://www.bianymeans.com/.

TUESDAY. Advent is All About Light.
Kate Kennington Steer

Advent is all about light: the absence of it and the glory of it. It is a season dear to my heart because I am a photographer who spends what seems like a lot of time waiting for the "right" light, and because I have spent a fair proportion of my life in the "darkness" of a chronic illness and under the pall of clinical depression.

November skies (and February skies for that matter) often seem to be characterised by a dullness, a heaviness, a flatness. The light seems stuck all day. I am learning to try to see this as "pearlescent" and "soft," where shadows are only hinted at, and colours can sometimes appear more "true." But after years of medication, this middling place is somewhere I have come to distrust, associating it with blankness and lack of sensation, with a cotton-woolled head to go with the massed banks of soft cloud.

So Advent's revelation often seems to coincide (in the south of England that is) with clearer, brisker weather that makes my soul sing out. If I am not well enough to venture out with my camera, I return to my habit of taking pictures out of windows. Then the light around my house seems to illuminate

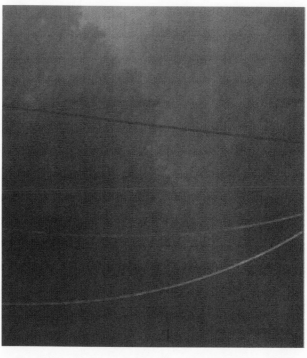

humdrum functional objects and treat them to a twist of mystery and majesty. My eyes seem to open wider in response to the angle of the sun as it travels lower in the sky. I am no longer so intimidated by a sun that sometimes stares so balefully, revealing the flaws in everything it touches. This low sun, though capable of spilling dramatic shadows hither and thither, seems to adopt Emily Dickinson's way of truth-telling that I have always found comforting: "tell the truth/but tell it slant."

Such angles of illumination seem a far cry from the blast of Advent glory-light that is often triumphantly used to characterise our God as Judge of all. I suspect that in our black-and-white blinkeredness, we mistake all glory-light as harsh. We cannot look straight into its heart, true, but I wonder if it is our lack of compassion for others as well as ourselves that means most of us cannot truly imagine what a Godly love-light might feel like to our soul. Yet this message of light in the Advent story is of the "both now and indeed then" kind. Incarnational light is precisely and absolutely everyday light: the ordinary, sometimes sunny, but mostly behind the clouds kind; the light that requires waiting for, in expectation of its sudden appearance, with hope. It is a sign of my own receding darkness that I am beginning to grasp (though oh so slowly) that revelations by this kind of light keep happening, whether I see them or not. My hope and prayer is that I might be given more of a glimpse, of more of those glints in God's eyes, more often.

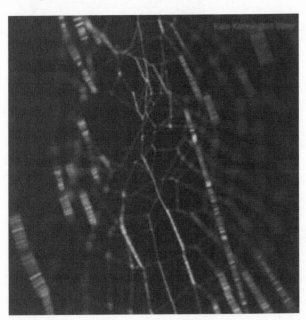

So perhaps the skies don't clear, and the weather doesn't actually change, has never really changed in December where I live. Perhaps it is rather that my Advent preoccupation with the Light makes me appreciate my everyday light differently, and remember it from year to year as a season when I might see more clearly, where my shadows are more clearly defined, and so healed; as a time when the work of Christ in me begins anew; as a prescribed period for reminding myself where and why I live. Advent is the place where I know I am a child of the Light.[32]

Kate Kennington Steer is a writer and photographer with a deep abiding passion for contemplative photography and spirituality. She writes about these things on shotattenpaces.blogspot.co.uk.

---

[32] To view Kate Kennington Steer's photographs as they originally appeared on *Godspace*, please visit her post there on December 4, 2013.

WEDNESDAY. Risky Invitations.
Mary Bergida

"You can't pick him. He's on his cell phone," I hiss at Miko.

It was too late. Miko strolls toward the bench on the plaza lawn. A frowning Asian student with a fringy mustache presses his phone to his ear.

I give a tentative smile at the student on the bench.

Miko offers a beaming smile and a flat palm waive. The student lowered the phone from his ear. His eyes tightened on our faces. Assessing us.

I want to absorb into the scraggly Florida grass beneath my flip-flops. I have always been sensitive and I am afraid we are about to make this student angry. When I was a child, my sensitivity revolved around being left out. I wasn't invited to the boy-next-door's birthday party because "it was stuff I wasn't big enough to do." Or in college, when my basketball-player boyfriend hadn't invited me to a Rock Star Party. "I just didn't think you'd come to something like that." He responded to my hurt. *Why didn't you ever even ask me?!* I had thought. But now, several years out of college, as a full-time missionary to college students, here was a student whose down-turned eyes, fumblings with his phone, are clear.

"Hey," says the student, almost menacingly.

Miko cheerfully launches into explaining that we are Missionaries from the Catholic Student Center on Campus here at the University of Florida, "UF." And wonders if he, the student, would be interested in taking our informal survey. Miko and I are in our second year as missionaries, engaging hundreds through spiritual surveys. Questions about everything from where they found happiness on campus to what they considered the greatest evil the world. These surveys are a springboard for inviting those interested in exploring God and spirituality to learn more. The rest of our missionary time is packed with leading Bible studies and doing student mentorship. These interactions seem natural and safe. However, these survey exploits always make me light-headed.

The student gives a flat grin, "Sure, I'm George, by the way."

Today, our survey poses questions to him about how his classmates, and he himself, explore faith while here at UF.

George explains that he was raised going to Church, but that God wasn't real for him.

I seize this as an invitation to connect. Tucking a curl behind my ear, I launch into my testimony about personally experiencing God in my own college days. I share how the trauma of a losing a family member was the portal through which God touched me. Found me.

Then I notice George's response. His face seems a blend of repulsion, boredom, perhaps frustration. Had we read him wrong?

I stop my story. My own fear and imagination see him stand and yell: "I wish you were at the bottom of the campus lake, with the gators."

I was right, Miko, this kid is not interested in talking about God, I think. I struggle for the words of a polite exit. Drag Miko away with me before we push George even farther away.

As I step back, George says quietly: "My freshman year, I looked for a Catholic Bible study and couldn't find one. I was just thinking about that last week."

Miko and I try to hide surprise. *What?*

In the next few weeks, George attends a Bible study and then goes on a student retreat. After the retreat, he looks me in the eyes. It's like a dead light bulb in him has been replaced. "Hi Mary!" He hugs me.

I am splashed with guilt. What if Miko had listened to me? What if I had decided not to bother George?

After that, I go out to "survey" and think of it as an invitation. Someone could always say no to us. No to talking about God.

But I still receive opposition, though externally, this time. Many peers and other missionaries tell me. "You Florida missionaries are too bold. People don't want to be bothered."

But time and time again, these words of caution are disproved.

One morning we again go out to meet and survey students. I approach a curly-haired girl, sitting under a tree. Above, feathery moss swings in the breeze. She tells us she has never been to a Church. But adds, "I want to know about God. I just need someone to tell me."

Several months later, Miko and I are out "surveying" again. We sit in the grass while a student rolls cigarettes and smokes them one after another. He excitedly shares with us his views on immortality. And then his friend rolls up on a bicycle. We summarize what we were talking about. Then invite him into the conversation by asking: "Who is God for you?"

The newly arrived friend, Chad, begins to tell us God is something he has given some hefty thought to. And that he had learned there is no God. He had spent the prior summer on an internship in Egypt working with a mathematician on a quest to scientifically explain the existence of God. But the project was unsuccessful. Suddenly, Chad throws his bike helmet to across the plaza grass.

He yells: "Do we have to talk about this? I want to go to lunch." I could hear my heart echoing his yells.

You are being yelled at, I realize in slight terror. But I don't back more to leave.

Silent seconds stretch out. Then more hushed, Chad adds, "I've tried to believe, but I can't."

We sit motionless. Looking up at him. At the helmet thrown across the plaza. Assure him we hadn't meant to upset. He should go get lunch.

He took some deep breaths, "Sorry, thanks guys for being so nice."

Before he and his cigarette-rolling friend head to Mo's for lunch, Chad gives Miko his phone number so they could meet up to eat hot wings and continue the conversation. We don't know if he will answer Miko's text to meet up, continue the conversation.

As we walk away, my legs are shaking. Recovering from the violence of Chad's reaction. We had made someone feel anger today, and we had come through. As we walk to our own lunch, I look at dozens of students sunbathing, biking past, headphones plugging their ears. What would happen if we could invite each of them to dialogue? Which ones were searching? Which bursting to share their frustration? Which waiting not to be left out?

I see now that both the "inviter" and the "invited" must accept vulnerability. The first to make invitations to meet and celebrate a Savior, Jesus Christ, were angels. They interrupted the ordinary lives of teenage Mary, scared Joseph, bored Shepherds. I hardly think of angels as sensitive or scared like me. Here I am, barely winged and hallowed, but somehow the modern bearer of tidings of great joy. The first Advent and all Advents are seasons of invitations. We so easily extend invites to Christmas parties and caroling. What if we pause in the flurry and make a bolder, more creative invite?

What if we decide that this season of Advent is forty days of letting go of judgment? How? What if I invite my agnostic friend to hear the Christmas story, either read at a Christmas party or Church service? I could ask my closet-Christian coworker to share what Christmas means to him. I'll call a homebound woman back in Florida and offer to read her Luke 2:1-20. And I'm going to keep thinking about who and how to invite—especially those who seem uninterested or easy to forget. And I invite you to do the same.

Mary Bergida had five and a half years of adventures as a full-time missionary with FOCUS (Fellowship of Catholic University Students). Now she is in her second year of earning her Master's in Creative writing from Seattle Pacific University, a journey of one word after another. She finds Jesus often inviting her to know him better through Lectio Divina and Ignatian/Imaginative prayer. Mary invites you to Google those.

LONGEST NIGHT. Winter Solstice.
Christine Sine

For many, this season is anything but cheerful, even when we have not had to put up with nonstop Christmas music for days beforehand. For all of us who have lost loved ones for whom we still grieve, lost a job, are struggling financially or with illness, this is not an easy season. And for those who have lost their houses and livelihoods due to natural disasters or war, the season will probably be anything but cheerful, so why do we try to cover our pain and grief with Yuletide cheer?

Many churches have begun to recognize that Festivals of Carols, celebrations of Christmas, and children's pageants do not meet everyone's needs. To fill this gap, churches offer a Blue Christmas service, a Service of Solace or Longest Night. People who are not having a very merry Christmas and friends who support them are invited to come and sit with one another in a liturgy that speaks of the love of God for the grieving.

St Andrew's Episcopal Church in Seattle holds a Blue Christmas celebration each year. The service includes a liturgy of remembrance with the lighting of four candles. The first candle is lit to remember those whom we have loved and lost. We pause to remember their name, their face, their voice, the memory that binds them to us in this season. The second candle is lit to redeem the pain of the loss of someone who was very important to us, part of our lives, part of our own selves. We pause to gather up the pain of the past and offer it to God, asking that from God's hands we receive the gift of peace. The third candle is to remember ourselves. We pause and remember the weeks and months of disbelief, the anger, the down times, the poignancy of reminiscing, the hugs and handshakes of family and friends, all those who stood with us. We give thanks for the support we have known. The last candle is to remember our faith and the gift of hope that the Christmas story offers us. We remember that God, who shares our life, promises us a place and time of no more pain and suffering.

—Christine

A Prayer for Longest Night

On this long dark night we await the coming of Christ.
We long for the light of his presence,
With us and in us.

When our souls are deeply troubled,
and our hearts break with the weight of sorrow,
may our grief be seasoned with love,
and our sorrow be buoyed by hope.

In our times of God-forsakenness and estrangement,
May we gaze on the innocent One,
made perfect through suffering.
and see in him our vulnerable God,
who saves in weakness and pain.

May our suffering empty us of pride,
and lead us to true joy,
our only security,
in Christ the infinite depths
of God's grace.

—Christine

Last year, I wrote my own prayer to help me through this season as I continue to grieve the loss of my mother; more Blue Christmas resources are available under the "Resources" tab at *msaimagine.org.*

Christine Sine is the Executive Director of Mustard Seed Associates. She trained as a physician in Australia and developed the medical ministry for Mercy Ships. She now speaks on issues relating to changing our timestyles and lifestyles to develop a more spiritual rhythm for life. She has authored several books including Return to Our Senses: Reimagining How We Pray; Godspace: Time for Peace in the Rhythms of Life; *and* Tales of a Seasick Doctor. *Christine blogs at* http://godspace-msa.com.

THURSDAY. Jesus is Coming—I Expect More Time. *Ed Cyzewski*

Nine years ago, we were newlyweds. I remember when our photo album arrived from the photographer with 4×6 prints and negatives. Yes kids, people actually used to hold pictures in their hands, and you could only make another print if you brought the negative to a developer—I'm sorry if all of this is making your head spin.

I looked through the pictures and began to think about having some prints made, buying frames, and putting up some pictures around the house. Perhaps a nice picture of Julie for my desk and a portrait in our bedroom.

However, I had seminary classes, my wife was attending graduate school, and it seemed like we never found the time for it. We'd wait for later—a time when we'd have more time.

Nine years later, I've made no progress on this. Worse than that, there are so many things that I've put off by telling myself, "I'll get to this when I have more time."

It's like I've created this fairy land in my future where I'll be rested, relaxed, and completely at leisure to do as I please. The truth is that we can always fill up our time with something. You can never have "enough" time.

One area where God is working on my heart lately is the stewardship of my time and how badly I can waste it. One night I drove over to our community market, which is an amazing natural foods/organic grocery co-op. It's in the middle of our residential neighborhood, so I parked on the street and could see the lights from televisions flashing in every single living room on our block.

The sight saddened me, but then God, champion for hypocrisy exposure, reminded me that I was chomping at the bit to go home and watch a bit of hockey. There was no use arguing that hockey is morally superior and more redemptive than Dancing with the Stars, even if I know that's true. The matter was one of time and priorities.

I can always put off important things by saying that I'll have more time in the future for them. This is a lie that turns me into the victim of the circumstances, when in reality I'm a victim of my own mismanagement—which is another way of saying that it's my fault alone.

When Jesus came to earth, Simon and Anna proclaimed that God's salvation had come that day. Herod sought to kill the newborn child because the threat to his rule was immediate. When God acts, there is no room for delay. We can't let our circumstances become obstacles.

Jesus told his disciples that the time has come now. Today is the day to repent. Today is the day to follow him. When a man tried to put off following Jesus in order to take care of his family obligations, Jesus wouldn't let him off the hook.

God's timeframe is always now, not later. As much as I'd like to delay dealing with my sins and bad habits, God wants to heal them now. As much as I'd like to fill my day up with "important" tasks, God wants me to pray now. Whenever God prompts us to act or sit, to think or rest, he's seeking what's best for us.

I keep thinking that I'll get to these things, but if I expect God to heal me in the future, he's actually saying that he wants to do it now. He doesn't want me to wait for a day when I'll be less busy, less stressed out, and less fragmented because that day will never come. While I wait for life to become less stressful, I miss out on the source of healing that I need the most—the one thing that I've been waiting for.

Ed is a freelance writer in Columbus, Ohio, advocate for sustainable discipleship, and author of the books Coffeehouse Theology *and* A Path to Publishing. *He thinks his house rabbits are way cooler than your cat. This essay was first posted on his blog* inamirrordimly.com.

FRIDAY. Surrounded by God's Grace: A Story of Fear and Friendship, Then and Now, *Kellie Carrara*

The surrounding glow of bright white lights encapsulated me as I watched the scurrying about below. Mechanical, buzzing noises hummed in a controlled panic. A blur of white-coated doctors and scrub-dressed nurses rushed in and out of the sterile room, tending to the scared young woman, wrapped in a thin, standard-issue gown.

Sensing her fear, I saw her pale face grow increasingly sad, tears streaming down. She was left alone, albeit abandoned in the cold room with white walls and medical equipment. Then, the door flung open, a man wearing confusion and concern, dressed in khaki twills and a fleece jacket shook the snow from his shoulders. Seeing his wife, he rushed to her side and took her hand. Not long after, another white-coated doctor entered the room; this time more slowly. His speech was muffled, but it was clear the news he delivered was devastating to the couple. He left, leaving the young couple to their grief as I helplessly continued to watch high above them, as if a dramatic movie played out before me.

Seeing this, perceiving their sadness, I felt nothing. I was merely a witness. I empathized at that moment, but did not share in their grief. The depth of their depression, one laced with murdered hopes and dreams of a new life, would come later. But at that moment, I was cradled in the arms of God, comforted by a wondrous protector.

Days passed and the reality of my first miscarriage set in, leaving me feeling empty and alone, yet in that moment in the hospital emergency room, God shielded me from the emotional impact.

I would have another miscarriage, and eventually a healthy pregnancy, resulting in a perfect baby daughter. And throughout each pregnancy, I not only felt God's love, but was gifted by good friends, who I could lean on. Enduring friendships that shared in my sadness, then my fears, then the excitement of the upcoming birth.

These friends showered me with good wishes and gifts of warm blankets and tiny clothes.

A talented artist friend designed and painted my nursery. My husband reminded me to eat the right things and lovingly watched me grow in the glow of pregnancy.

When the time of impending arrival dawned, my mother and best friend, two wonderfully strong women, sat patiently beside me, encouraging me through hours of labor, urging me onward. They were the first to witness my miracle, my Mira.

Friends streamed in and out of a brightly lit room, this time filled with happiness, love, warmth and the sweet chirpings of a newborn. Nurses tended to my every need. Allowing me rest, giving me comfort, sheltering me from any intrusions, keeping everything that entered my sacred room clean.

Days later, once in our home, family and friends continued to visit with gifts of hot food, baby necessities and congratulations. I never felt alone. God had seen me through and had given me friends here on earth.

Yet when I reflect on Mary, I can hardly fathom the emptiness she must have felt throughout her pregnancy and through the early years of motherhood.

How her own friends and family must have reacted to her pregnancy. Unplanned. Unexplained. Did she hide it as long as she could, under layers of clothing, suffering alone and in fear? Leaning on God, His infinite wisdom and guidance, as I had, through my own fears?

Once her secret was out, did her friends turn on her? Talk behind her back? What of her own family? Did they soothe her fears or question her morals? Did they focus on her future and that of the young baby or dwell on her unknown and suspected past actions?

How scared she must have felt when she told her betrothed Joseph! When he turned away from her, seemingly on the verge of a breakup, with thoughts of ruin and poverty in her future.

Though Joseph came back and believed Mary, taking her as promised to be his wife, what did they then endure together? What of his own friends? What did they think of him marrying a pregnant girl? Where was his own support network? More than 2,000 years later, I can only imagine rumors and speculation ran rampant and the two faced months of ridicule.

Was it a welcome quiet and relief to leave town and travel to Bethlehem so close to the baby's birth? Fraught with fears of the long distance of rugged, bumpy terrain, Mary jostled atop the slow-moving donkey, with Joseph beside her, fearful of roadside bandits and dangerous animals along the way. Suffering through hours of hot sun, dust storms and endlessly narrow roads, they pressed on toward their destination. I imagine prayers were uttered throughout the journey.

With no one to take her hand and lead her to a fresh, clean birthing bed, not a knowledgeable soul to guide her through unexpected, foreign pains of labor, she still remained steadfast. Joseph, himself, must have been overcome with newfound fears and concern.

She must have been thirsty…and hungered for guidance and emotional strength as she made her final push. Who was there to wrap the tiny miracle and place Him in His mother's arms, as the nurses so lovingly did for me?

Utterly exhausted, I imagine the relief and joy they felt…a primal euphoria of new parents. Meanwhile, word was out of the miraculous arrival, and dirty field workers made their way into town to view the new king. Originally thought of as Jesus' welcoming committee, I wonder if they were nothing more than gawkers, ancient paparazzi merely wanting a first glimpse of a would-be celebrity.

Did they rush the stable, filthy from the fields, craning their necks to see Him? How did Mary and Joseph feel? Did they lift him up and show him off or shield him from the unknown men?

Still alone in her recovery and exhaustion of motherhood, who was there to help with the new teachings? Provide a hot meal, fresh cloth for diapers and spit up? How long was the couple to stay in their current conditions? And surely soon they learned their safety was in question, and realized they could not return home to family and comfort. Alone again, and afraid. Clinging to each other and their new baby, having little money and no one to turn to, they became a homeless family on the run. They grew dependent on the generosity of strangers, keeping their new son hidden, lest he be slaughtered by the order of the current king.

How is it that Mary, a young woman who so desperately needed and longed for earthly friendship and support, comfort and guidance would in turn bring up a son to be the greatest friend an entire world would know and depend on forever?

When she, herself, needed friends the most, she turned to but the one guiding strength she knew. Her God and His Son.

In the end, it would be her baby, Jesus, that would give her life meaning and purpose by His very birth. A gift He would go on to give nations for all eternity.

Ironic that when all feels lost—all earthly love, support and comfort is gone, there is but one friend who will always love, support and comfort. No matter the time in life, in giving new life, in grieving for lost life, but for life. Forever.

Kellie Carrara lives near Boston with her husband and daughter. She is a former newspaper reporter, turned fashion and advertising copywriter, who also produces fashion television segments across the U.S.

CHRISTMAS EVE. The Night Before.
Joel Boehner

Last night a snow fell
that softened sharp edges,
filled in holes, and brought
a few tall things lower.

Yet, some today are frozen,
some drifted into ditches.
I remember where I was
the day you were born.

When I shoveled the walk,
I saw your face through the
window, through two panes:
already but not yet.

Joel wrote this poem on the occasion of his then foster daughter's first birthday. He and his wife, Anne, have since adopted Alyssa. They live in South Bend, Indiana, and worship at Keller Park Missionary Church.

SATURDAY. *Gather, Feast, Create*

Gather

Depending on which day Christmas Eve falls, gathering as a community group may not be feasible. Whether you meet together or not this week, keep things simple. Consider using either of Christine's prayers for Blue Christmas or Christmas Eve at the end of your time. One way to capture the building excitement for Christmas and serve people who often find themselves feeling especially lonely at this time of year is to round up a group of neighbors or other friends from your community and go Christmas caroling at a local nursing home. Don't be shy about your musical ability! Your songs will be greatly appreciated by your listeners.

Feast

Meal: Cocoa, snacks, cookies, and appetizer potluck

If caroling is in your plans this evening, bring along favorite snacks, cookies, appetizers, and a carafe of hot cocoa or cider to share. Consider making extra batches and dividing them into plastic bags to share with the local homeless population or shelter.

Create

As a group, plan ahead to bring a selection of items that may be grouped and placed into plastic bags and distributed to panhandlers. This is a great way to get children involved in doing something tangible for people who are homeless. Tubes of lip balm, pairs of new socks, travel-sized toothpaste or lotion, new toothbrushes, and granola bars can be placed in piles on a table or counter top and placed into quart- or gallon-sized plastic bags assembly-line style. If you would like to be more eco-conscious with your packaging, use one sock of a pair as the "bag" and place the other gift items as well as the second sock inside. Keeping a number of these bags in your car will give you something to pass on to panhandlers, who are in need of these items more urgently in the winter. Don't forget to look your neighbor in the eye when you pass along your gift! Donating new or gently used blankets, coats, and sleeping bags to a local shelter is another fine idea to remember your neighbors during the cold months of the northern hemisphere.

—Kristin

O ORIENS

"O Radiant Dawn, splendor of eternal light, sun of justice: Come, shine on those who dwell in darkness and the shadow of death."

Christmas

[Image: Rural village in Iraq]

O Radiant Dawn

Shout
to the nations,
sing to the whole earth,
The Eternal One reigns!
The world is anchored by his presence
and will not shake loose.
So, let the heavens resound in gladness!
Let joy be the earth's rhythm
as the seas and all its creatures roar.
Let the fields grow in triumph
a grand jubilee for all that live there.
Let all the trees of the forest dig in and reach high
with songs of joy before the Eternal one.
For Christ our saviour the One who is faithful and true
has come.
His throne was established from the beginning of the world.
He will set the world right by his truth and justice.
His righteousness and peace and wholeness
will last through all eternity.

(Adapted from Psalm 96).

Now that Christmas Day is over, many of us feel let down because the day we have been anticipating for so long is over. The malls strip their elaborate decorations and junk their remaining Christmas stocks with huge 50-70%-off sales. The Christmas wreaths and trees are thrown out for the garbage collectors and our frenzied activities give way to a low-grade depression. But Christmas isn't really over. In the sixth century, it was decided that celebrating Christmas just for a day didn't provide time to celebrate all the joy that Christ's birth brought into the world. They made Christmas into a twelve-day festival that ended with a feast on the Eve of Epiphany on January 5th to celebrate the coming of the wise men. Yep, that's right! The twelve days of Christmas begin with Christmas Day; they don't end there as many malls would have us believe. In countries where this understanding of Christmas has not been co-opted by the commercialism of our society, Christmas trees are not decorated until Christmas Eve and remain in the house sparking with light and life until the Eve of Epiphany.

This is the season when we are meant to celebrate with joy and gratitude the wonder of a God whose love is so great that he sent his son to dwell amongst us. How incredible! How wonderful! Let's take advantage of every day of the Christmas season.

—Christine

Prayers for Christmas

God we welcome your bright and shining star.
Let us not be distracted,
or turned aside by busyness or power.

Let us bow before your Son.
A child born in a manger,
A son sent to redeem the world,
A savior come to renew all things.

Let us rejoice with him,
Cast off the works of darkness,
And put on the ways of light.
The light of God's morning star be on you,
The light of Christ's redeeming love be in you,
The light of the Spirit's sustaining presence shine through you,
in this season of new birth.

Through Advent we have watched and waited.
In Christmas we have found the Messiah,
and we have been changed.
Now we must follow God's guiding star,
light to the world, redemption for all people.

We can no longer be satisfied with the old life.
We must journey deeper into God.

May we open our ears to listen,
so that we can hear God's heartbeat.
May we open our eyes to watch,
so that we can see God's presence.
May we open our minds to believe,
so that we can embrace God's ways.
May we open our hearts to trust,
so that we can share God's salvation.

—Christine

FIRST DAY OF CHRISTMAS.
December 25. Shhh...Here He Comes!
Margaret Magi Trotman

Shhhh...here he comes! Or shhhh! He's coming!

What if it was a surprise party and everyone in the whole WORLD was invited?! Don't "shush" the party goers...Lead them to the mountaintops, the rooftops, the treetops, and SHOUT, for joy "HERE HE COMES!!" Like the song says..."Go tell it on the mountain...and everywhere!" (One of my personal favorite Christmas songs.)

Let us stop for a moment and put on the hats of our childhood. Forget the meetings and noise, the responsibilities and logic. When life wasn't looked upon as a science but was really just happy approximates? Let us look at the world through new old eyes. Remember? How we watched the process with wonder? When "are we there yet?" meant how much time do I have left to dream in the scenery passing by? The magic of anticipation with joyous eyes and knowing smile when cookies glowed under the burner inside the oven rose then settled like a deflating bed of sweet bubbling goodness. Even if you were a child on a farm, or helped in a garden, you knew...that waiting was all the best part of getting to the goal. Watching eggs hatch, a goat born or a crop grow; it's all in God's good time when we are all born. Our father would tell us to wait and be still, we would answer merely "Okay" and sit in stillness and wonder as God worked his miracles right before our eyes.

Look now through your eyes as a child at how the easy faith in just knowing creates a peace our hearts that Christmas was meant to bring. I remember the joy of the lights of Christmas, the gifts of course, but there was another feeling I always had. I, even as a child, would become emotional and silent, almost overwhelmed with the presence that surrounded me. I liked Santa and the pretty papers and especially the songs, but I knew also, inherently, this Gift to mankind in the form of a baby human.

I was allowed to uncover the baby's statue in the crèche on Christmas morning and did so with such care, as if not to awaken him. This child, asleep after such a long journey here, so long ago, has never left, even now. This child, who knew

141

where his life would lead him, where his Father would lead him. This child, born to us, simply. Waited for his time of completion and perfection...as do we.

Magi describes herself as a child of God first, an artist and writer married to a former Marine, with whom she shares a farm in northeast Florida. They have several four-legged, feathered, shelled and scaled babies. Off the farm are their grown children and not so grown grand-boys and girls who they find extremely awesome. Magi enjoys photography, reading, composing handwritten letters, making her own cards. She says, "life is good because God gave it to us and us to each other."

(Nativity, Gertrud Kasesbier 1901)

SECOND DAY OF CHRISTMAS.
December 26. Feast Day of St. Stephen.
It Has Come to This. *Dave Timmer*

It Has Come to This

Why do you forget
What it is that I said
A blessing to my creation
But your self-interest instead

You strive for more power
And pile up rules to follow
But it's your heart that matters
And you've made it so shallow
You've cursed yourselves

With law and oppression
Listen to my prophets
Who hint at redemption
Mercy and Justice

It is this I require
The revenge that you seek
Only thickens the mire
It has come to this

As I continually pursue
Even the rocks cry out
I will come to show you
In the darkness so heavy

Into an empire so strong
The light still flickers
But for a king you still long
Mary's song—a revolution

And the mighty are stilled
But you still don't understand
That the hungry will be filled

A new kind of kingdom
The blind they will see
The prophecy is fulfilled
Now come follow me

You are forgiven
Dropping their rocks you'll see
Their names in the dust
Now it is just you and me
As you look forward today

Just remember this
Mercy and Justice
Were betrayed with a kiss
The curtain was torn down

Through a death so gory
It's now time to come home to
The great redemption story
And some millennia later

The church still stands
But it has often forgotten
The work of My hands
You are so much like them

Through all humanity
You've made an idol
Of your own security
So another voice yells out—

If you believe he has risen
Stop waiting for something
That has already been given
My story is for everyone

Your piety will only hinder
And my Kingdom unfurls
Through Peace now consider
All creation is groaning
As you strive for more power

144

I am still with you
But you need to look lower

With the poor and the lowly
The good news is sent
The prisoner is set free
And the crippled are not bent

The Messiah incarnate
The crumbling mountains don't miss
The wine flowing jubilantly
It has again come to this[33]

Dave is Director for A Rocha USA in northwest Washington. Dave farms on A Rocha's small urban farm called Five Loaves Farm, helps organize the Lynden Farmers Market, works on watershed restoration projects, and studies the ecology of Cascadia. A Rocha has recently begun renting a beautiful property just outside of Lynden, Washington, that they will farm, study, and host interns.

---

[33] Editor's note: St. Stephen's Day commemorates the first known Christian martyr. Stephen's story is found in the Acts of the Apostles, Chapter 7, where he makes a speech before his death, having been accused of the crime of blasphemy.

THIRD DAY OF CHRISTMAS.
December 27. Feast Day of St. John the Evangelist. Pancha Rathas,
Amanda Stevens

3

This piece was inspired during my time spent studying abroad in India after a visit to monolithic stone temples sitting on the southeast coast of India named Pancha Rathas, which were part of a 7th-century port city called Mahabalipuram. As groups of tourists were walking toward the temples, I noticed two beggars: one female, one male, both crippled and elderly sitting on each side of the pathway. Based on this moment, I wrote this poem to help myself process my thoughts on poverty in India and the tension of wondering if the structure of society as it is now could ever allow for poverty to cease. But as I've been reflecting on what it means to observe and wait for the coming of Christ, especially the Second Coming that we also celebrate and prepare for during Advent; I realized that though originally this piece was written specifically about the ancient pain of poverty, I think that it also uniquely illustrates that sense of waiting for redemption, for all to be made well. It is depicting that moment in between Christ's coming which brought redeeming hope and Christ's second coming when we will finally, fully, at last step into that redemption.

Pancha Rathas

A goat kid sleeps on a dancing statue:
turquoise worn and paused in-step,
one foot raised and waiting
to feel the slap against the stone.
It seems all hang on that final
beat, even the monolith temples
wait for their builders' return,
when they'll bow against the
sanded floors in narrow openings
between corridors.
And outside the city wait the cross-
legged guards, crazed and cloudy-eyed,
as vacant and indifferent as the sun
gathering in the pavement and beating

through their bones. But for their disfigured hands;
alive enough to open to the movement
in passing crowds of silhouettes and footsteps,
and hang in the air for the drop of a coin—
for the turn of its fated faces.

Amanda Stevens is a former Mustard Seed Associates summer intern. She works in the field of special education/respite; while also pursuing her love for creative expression in her free time. Her work has recently been published in an upcoming ebook anthology entitled Poetic Reflections.

Hans Memling, St. John the Evangelist on Patmos, public domain

FOURTH DAY OF CHRISTMAS.
December 28. Holy Innocents Day. The Innocents Still Among Us. *Cindy Spencer*

4

Over the years, our family has made a practice of really trying to keep Advent and the 12 Days of Christmas, to hold off on our celebration, and to fully prepare and enter this great mystery that somehow God became a human person, knowing and redeeming us from the inside out through participation in the physicality of life. Even with time spent in preparation, it is easy to sentimentalize the Christmas story. Babies, after all, are beautiful, innocent and trusting, and stories about babies, and especially about *this* baby, as often told in church school pageants, make even the rough circumstances of this birth seem sweet and sometimes precious. And our home practice is full of good, and often sentimental, things—time together as a family, candlelit worship services on Christmas Eve, singing favorite Christmas hymns and carols, of favorite foods and family traditions.

And then, today, on the fourth day of Christmas, just as we're getting into the swing of the twelve days, the Feast of the Holy Innocents comes along. There's just really nothing sentimental, warm or comforting about this part of the story, where an insecure and jealous Herod, who is unable to determine exactly which young boy the Magi where seeking, takes it upon himself to kill them all, just to be sure his political position is safe. And while we rejoice that Jesus had already escaped to Egypt, thanks to an angelic warning and the quick action of Mary and Joseph, we mourn for the children, the mothers and fathers, and we wonder why it was allowed to happen this way. This scene provides us with a psychic break—it jars us, discomforts us, and calls us to recall that all is not sweetness and light simply because the Messiah, the baby who would change everything, has entered the world.

God entered the world, and we celebrate, and then we realize that his birth, and later his death and resurrection, didn't end human suffering. In our own time, over 2000 years after the birth of Christ, there are still Holy Innocents among us. Those who, because of the location of their birth, their race, or their social class, are considered acceptable collateral damage in the struggles for power and security that rage around us. In this past year, we might add the children of Gaza, the children of Central America seeking asylum at our borders, young black men in the wrong place at the wrong time. This day calls us to look squarely at those who are considered expendable in our own time and place.

In this way, the feast day of the Holy Innocents operates much like the call of the prophets we heard in early Advent (such a long time ago, now!) to consider that salvation is needed now, in this time and in this place, that injustice demands our attention, and has attracted the attention of the God who longs to save us. In the midst of our Christmas feast, we need to stop to see and consider how to share that feast with those we'd rather not even see in our midst.

In the Episcopal Church, in our baptismal covenant, we are asked "Will you seek and serve Christ in all persons?" What if, today, on the fourth day of Christmas, we intentionally pull our gaze from the baby in the manger and seek God in the faces of the Holy Innocents in our midst?

Cindy Spencer lives in Seattle where she is a wife, the mother of three young adults, and works with children and families at Saint Mark's Episcopal Cathedral and the Episcopal Diocese of Olympia. She occasionally blogs for Episcopal Lifelong, *a Christian formation blog, and loves keeping the seasons of the church year at home.*

FIFTH DAY OF CHRISTMAS.
December 29. Gifts of Light and Love, a Christmas Poem. *Heather Jephcott*

5

It's about giving
precious gifts
of thoughtfulness
gentleness
packaged with laughter
joy accompanying smiles

Delight filled faces
light up
receiving
gifts of love
an air of happiness surrounds
pleased with the giving

A grand party of giving
with everyone included
caring for needs
attentive to likes
unselfish consideration

Surprise adds an extra specialness
child-like wonder comes to visit
discovering again
love, joy, hope and peace

Heather comes from Australia but now lives in Surabaya Indonesia. She enjoys writing, especially poetry, playing the piano, friends and family, black line drawings, gardening, photography, reading. She also loves interacting with people...health or the lack of it has got in the way at times, but she's getting better after 17 years with Chronic Fatigue Syndrome. She never wants to be too busy for people. Heather is the author of a book of poetry, Open Hearts, Quiet Streams.

SIXTH DAY OF CHRISTMAS.
December 30. The Best Gifts for Christmas.
Steve Wickham

6

"The angel Gabriel said to Mary, 'The Holy Spirit will come upon you, and the power of the Most High will overshadow you; therefore the child to be born will be holy; he will be called Son of God'"
—Luke 1:35(NRSV).

Our modern culture has us lost to the Christmas story because of the hurry and bustle that entraps us as we approach it, and that, usually, for love. Motivation to get the planning done right—gifts selected, organised, and wrapped, preparations for feasts made, travel plans for incoming or outgoing family members booked, etc.—means we often lose sight of the wonder enfolded in the ancient Christmas story.

After all, the Saviour of the world was just being born; God's redemptive plan ignited.

An interesting thing occurs when we decide for reflection over busyness; even for intentionally dreamy moments sprinkled within chaos.

We get to enjoy the experience of true spirituality: joy, peace, and goodwill toward all. The greatest of gifts at Christmas time, or any time for that matter, are those of virtue; three are selected to illustrate:

1. Joy
It's only when we have space between the ears that we can envision and enter into joy. A hurried mind is beyond joy, but reflection over what we've experienced, survived from, and learned about through our year brings the quiet joy of satisfaction.

Besides, thought of Jesus is, as Isaac Watts put it, *Joy to the World*. But only as we draw near to Christmas with thought of Jesus do we gain access to such joy.

2. Peace
Peace may very well result from joy; and hope is not too distant an experience, either. If joy is made available when we have time to think, how much more is peace?

151

We can only experience peace, commencing from within, when we are not at war with anything. Conflicts have been resolved. But, the materialistic temptation of typical Western Christmas nowadays separates us from such peace and even forges conflict. Will we be drawn into it this year?

3. Goodwill (grace)
How wonderful to enjoy those wondrous gifts at Christmas: joy and peace. How could they not propagate goodwill between us and our loved ones, and friends, and neighbours?

Christmas is about the birth of Jesus; the physical commencement of the reconciliatory age. How much better to emulate such redemptive philosophy within one's own family? Forgiveness abides perfectly at Christmas time.

The best of practical blessings is freely available during the Christmas season. Those blessings well over in freely-flowing love as family and close friends celebrate the wonder of Jesus' birth in a spirit of harmonious, thanks-filled fellowship.

All that Christmas is about is Jesus. If we remember that, reflecting over it in humble gratitude, we may gain joy, peace, and goodwill to carry us through the season—we will never be better blessed.

© 2011 S. J. Wickham.

Steve is a regular contributor to Godspace *from Perth, Australia. He is a Baptist pastor who holds degrees in science, divinity, and counseling. He blogs at* Epitome *and* Tribework.

SEVENTH DAY OF CHRISTMAS.
December 31. New Year's Eve. Inquire Within. *Monette Chilson*

7

At this week's Religion Newswriters Association conference, Clifford Saron referenced a University of Virginia study—reported by *Science Magazine* this past summer—that, astoundingly, found that people would rather administer an electrical shock to themselves than sit alone and meditate.[34] Really? How do we get to a point, as a culture, that we prefer physical pain to quiet contemplation? What are we afraid of?

Over the past decade, my spiritual expression has evolved from outward (worship) to inward (contemplation). Singing and verbose prayers overstimulate me. They drown out the quiet whisper that I am training my soul to hear. When someone says, "Let us pray," and then uses words to fill the sacred silence, I am taken aback. I have become quite the spiritual introvert.

We, in the West, are obsessed with the takeaway. So, what do I get out of all this silence? Well, it depends on the day. It depends on what God needs to teach me. This week, in the silence, I realized that I was creating chaos and unrest in my life by overcommitting. Overcommitting to good and worthy pursuits, but overcommitting nonetheless. Without a quiet space to reflect, I would have forged ahead, my prayers a string of words, songs and good deeds, pulling me along, leaving me jangling like a tin can behind one of those just-married-mobiles.

Instead, the need to back off was revealed to me. I switched my list from a to-do list to an un-do list. Counterintuitively, I forced myself to cancel two things before delving into the litany of productivity running through my head. I had to create space before I could extend any further. If you practice yoga, you know that feeling well. Not "know" in an intellectual way, but "know" because you've moved it and breathed it. You've learned that to get length in your spine, you must first create space, and you must do it without harming yourself in the process (no low-back crunching).

---

[34] Nadia Whitehead, "People Would Rather be Electrically Shocked Than Left Alone With Their Thoughts, July 3, 2014, American Association for the Advancement of Science. http://news.sciencemag.org/brain-behavior/2014/07/people-would-rather-be-electrically-shocked-left-alone-their-thoughts.

In another meditative revelation, I realized that I was suffering from Cinderella Syndrome—that I was not allowing myself to go the ball until I had done all my work. What that looked like in my life was trying to fulfill all my outside obligations before giving myself permission to do the things that fulfill me, personally. We all know that if we wait until we've checked all those other

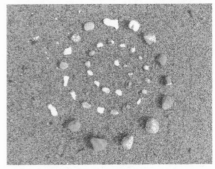

Photo credit Kristin Carroccino

things off our lists, we'll never get to the work of our heart. There will always be something to lure us away from the work that's dearest to us, the work that blurs the line between the earthly and the ethereal, bringing us just a little closer to God.

So today, inquire within. Listen. And heed the wisdom that emerges from the silence.

Namaste.

This piece first appeared on Monette's blog Sophia's Whispers *on September 19, 2014.*

Monette Chilson writes and speaks about using the Eastern practices of yoga and meditation to bring mindfulness to the Western religious experience. Her book, Sophia Rising: Awakening Your Sacred Wisdom Through Yoga *(Bright Sky Press, 2013), was awarded the Illumination Book Award gold medal, as well as the Hoffer Small Press and First Horizon Awards. Her work has appeared in* Yoga Journal, Integral Yoga Magazine, Elephant Journal, Om Times *and* Christian YogaMagazine. *Read more at* www.SophiaRisingYoga.com.

DECEMBER 31. *Gather, Feast, Create*

Gather

New Year's Eve is a time to celebrate the old year and the new, to party and to contemplate. As a group, find a labyrinth in your community and go together to walk it. At its center, leave behind a symbol of the past year and walk out of the labyrinth with fresh intentions for the new year. Or, gather around a fire and write down old habits you intend to leave behind on a piece of paper and place it in the fire to symbolize the possibilities of the months ahead. On another sheet of paper, write down hopes for the coming year and add them later to a journal or tape to a surface at home that you view regularly.

Feast

Meal: International foods potluck and/or Cake and beverages at midnight

Enjoy a dinner party with cuisine from around the world as you talk about the past year and the new year. If everyone is still gathered at midnight, or if you are returning from a labyrinth walk, celebrate with champagne or sparkling cider and cake!

Create

Choose a craft to do individually or as a group. Try drawing mandalas or making a collage together. For mandala ideas, visit http://www.art-is-fun.com/how-to-draw-a-mandala.html. For collages, collect photographs from the past year, cut them into shapes, and paste them onto a thick piece of paper. Add inspirational words, poems, or quotes to your collage.

—**Kristin**

EIGHTH DAY OF CHRISTMAS.
New Year's Day. On NOT Staying in my Cave. *Michael Yankoski*

8

Two weeks ago, sensing that my mental frenzy was reaching something of a fever pitch, I decided to make another retreat into a cave. I was quite excited for the time away, delighted to not have any network-connected devices with me, hopeful of finding a bit of a slower pace in order to be reminded again what a "resting heart rate" (as opposed to a "stressed-out"/"caffeinated-out heart rate") actually feels like.

When I first arrived at the mouth of the cave, I was panting from the climb up to the top of the ridge, full of endorphins and completely soaked with sweat. I slung off my pack, said a prayer of thanks for having been brought back all the way across the country, across the ocean, across the ridge in order to be back at the cave.

Then I slipped down into the cool darkness of the cave's interior.

As I knelt down in the cave to catch my breath, the memory of last year's week-long retreat in the cave [came] rushing back to me: my slow singing of songs late into the night, the candlelit recitation of millennium-old prayers, the mice and the bats whose daily and nightly rhythms I became more familiar with than I'd hoped with over the course of the week. I felt myself fill with the hope of a similar retreat.

But I was in for a surprise.

Delicious as the cool comfort and stillness of the cave were that afternoon, they didn't last long. In less than a minute, a cloud of mosquitoes had gathered about me, their incessant, high-pitched whine shockingly similar to the countless distractions that so often take me away from being truly mindful of the things I most deeply want to be attentive toward.

I debated for a few minutes whether remaining there amidst all these unexpected cave-dwellers would actually provide anything like the sort of retreat I'd envisioned.

While swatting away the twentieth mosquito, something snapped into focus for me: we don't often stumble upon stillness. It must be cultivated. Sought out. Pursued. Sometimes finding silence and stillness and solitude means changing

156

our well-laid plans and finding other ways to enter into the restoration we so badly need.

Once I'd come to see this, I stood upright again, climbed out of the cave, and retreated twenty minutes back down the ridgeline until a new setting for my retreat presented itself to me. I knew it as soon as I saw it: a gentle outcropping high atop a cliff, just beneath the colorful and crooked limbs of an old arbutus tree.

"This will be my Still Point," I said, throwing down my sleeping mat.

I set up camp, made a cup of tea, and watched with widened eyes as the moon rose up from beneath the eastern horizon. I listened to the sound of the swallows dipping and diving through the warm currents of air rising up along the cliff and slowly—thanks to the rush of wind in the trees and the sight of the ancient tides spilling back into the Sound far below me—began to feel my heart-rate and thought-rate and life-rate slow towards a more hopeful cadence.

I don't know when I'll have the chance to return to the cave again.
Nor to the ridge that was the setting for this most recent rejuvenation.

But as I get ready to transition away from these months on the West Coast, toward my current residence in Indiana, I'm carrying with me the clear conviction that life-drinking mosquitoes of all kinds will be waiting with their high-pitched whine, that silence must be cultivated, and sought out and protected, that I must find places and practices of stillness and silence and solitude if I'm to maintain anything like a Christ-centered approach to myself, to others, to the world in the coming year.

Lord have mercy…

Michael Yankoski is a writer, aspiring theologian and urban homesteader who dreams of one day becoming a competent woodworker, musician, potter and sailor. He is the author of Under the Overpass *and also* The Sacred Year. *(www.TheSacredYear.com). He and his wife Danae are both PhD students at the University of Notre Dame. More of his work may be found at* www.MichaelYonkoski.com.

NINTH DAY OF CHRISTMAS.
January 2. And Moved into the Neighborhood.
Jeri Bidinger

9

"And the Word became flesh, and made his dwelling among us" (John 1:14).

There is this story I tell. To my kids, to students, and as part of my story of what matters. I grew up outside the church in a family stuck in the muck of addictions and anger. When I was fifteen, some girls from school, urged on by a believing woman who chose to love me, tried to bring me into their circle. One day, several of us went to Krissy's house. There I sat, uncomfortable, an outsider to their laughter and confidence.

The phone rang. I could hear Krissy's mother's end of a conversation from the next room.

"Really? That's big—what a hard decision! No, I don't know what you should do. ... Hmmm, I don't know. But I'll pray for you. Yes, the Lord cares about this. Let's pray to know how to handle things. I'll call you again tomorrow."

The chatter, the giggles and teasing, my discomfort—all faded as I eavesdropped on that call. A mom who talked about God on the phone. A mom who prayed. A mom who thought prayer mattered, that Jesus might enter and show the way. In that moment, my whole world changed.

My usual talking point for this story is that we never know what goes on behind the doors of another's home, and we never know what profound impact our everyday actions of faith might have on lonely eavesdroppers in our homes.

"The Word became flesh" and moved to a new place. Jesus left his eternal home to make a temporary home in a place where no one knew him.

We find ourselves on the Mediterranean coast of Turkey. After living seven years in the Middle East. Not by accident. We were drawn here, invited, we believe, by that same Word who moved to physical Israel 2,000 years ago. Invited to purchase property and make space for people who seek solitude for prayer and rest. We call it "Spa for the Soul," and we moved here with intention.

But we soon understood that we also moved into a neighborhood, a community where no one had before encountered the Word enfleshed. As I write these lines, the mosque singer sings and his call echoes above the wind over the hillside. It penetrates our office and our bedroom and wafts down to the sea below. Twelve days into Advent and not a sign of Christmas anywhere.[35]

We understood we'd moved into the neighborhood, so we schooled ourselves to listen and to love. From earliest days, first one, and then a few more, and then others, called me Mommy. Their children call me *babaanne* or *anneanne* (father's mother or mother's mother) depending on which parent attached first. It surprised me. Still does. I looked for a cultural explanation, but found none. I listened to their stories and realized that many of these dear ones are distant from birth-family. Some have lost their parents. Others, well, there are stories from their growing-up years. All are met deeply by parental love.

Mother love. Attentive, accepting, forgiving. One who listens, treasures, helps, and on occasion is severe. One who takes time, who is interested. One who is present.

Can a mother forget the baby at her breast
and have no compassion on the child she has borne?
Though she may forget, I will not forget you!
See, I have engraved you on the palms of my hands;
your walls are ever before me (Isaiah 49:15-16).

Yes, we came with a purpose. But we also moved into a community. As the Word did 2,000 years ago. Incarnation. Jesus in human flesh. To make a home among these beloved ones, to invite them to our home, to let them hear us pray for them, to offer welcome to true and eternal homecoming.

And so in this season, we light the Advent candles and we put out a small nativity not too fragile to be played with. I prepare an old handmade cradle that we will put in the entryway, so that we can tell of an overfull house with place found for just one more, the Gift who makes space and welcome for us all. The One who invites us home to live with him.

---

[35] Editor's Note: Though this is an Advent piece, it was selected for Christmas to remind all of us to continue to "extend the table," keep up the Christmas feast, and always "make room" for one more.

Jeri Bidinger spends her days in the Mediterranean village of Gökseki, just outside of Kaş, Turkey, caring for whoever God brings. She and her husband Curt have created a contemplative retreat center there that they call Spa for the Soul. Jeri is a retired attorney, former BSF teaching leader, and spiritual director. She posts from time to time at www.crackedoldpots.blogspot.com, and looks forward to the publication of her book on Biblical gender, the first book written for Albanian Christians to be formally published in Albania. The rest of her time is given over to language study, serving guests in one way or another, loving on the community, and enjoying her family.

TENTH DAY OF CHRISTMAS.
January 3. Jesus is Returning…Today.
Jeremy Myers

10

No, I'm not pulling a "Harold Camping[36]." Though I do believe that Jesus will return to earth literally and physically at some time in the future, I am NOT saying that today is the day.

But I am saying that Jesus is returning today. And tomorrow. And the next day. And every day from now until He actually returns.

Confused yet? I am saying that Jesus returns daily until He actually returns.

THE DAILY RETURN OF JESUS?

I think that as Christians, we have often taught and thought about what Scripture says concerning the future return of Jesus Christ, while ignoring and neglecting what Scripture says concerning the present and daily return of Jesus Christ. If you didn't know that such an idea is taught in Scripture, then you have proved my point. Most people don't know it, which is why most people don't live for it.

Yet the idea of the daily return of Jesus Christ is quite prevalent in Scripture. Jesus talked about it in Acts 1 before He ascended into heaven. Paul talks about it in several of His letters as does Peter, James, and John.

During His three years of earthly ministry, Jesus served others by healing the sick, providing for the poor, loving the outcast, teaching the masses, feeding the hungry, delivering the captives, eating with sinners, partying with prostitutes, and in general, showing people what it looks like for God to be ruling and reigning on earth.

And then, after Jesus died and rose again from the dead, He basically told His followers:

You are my witnesses, my ambassadors to the world. The things you have heard me say? You now say similar things to the world. The things you have seen me do? You now do similar

---

[36] Editor's Note: Harold Camping was an American evangelist who predicted that the "end of the world" would happen on May 21, 2011.

things, or even greater things. The people you have seen me hang out with? You now hang out with them.

As you say these things, and do these things, and hang out with these people, know that I am there with you, in you and through you, saying these things and doing these things and loving these people all over again.

If I stay, I am only one person. But if I go, I can send my Spirit into each one of you, so that I can multiply myself in each one of you, and in you, be the voice of God, the touch of God, and the love of God to all people.

Many people today are hoping for change. Hoping for corruption to end. Hoping for greed to cease. Hoping for equality, mercy, freedom, and justice. And a large segment of people who hope for these things believe that such things will not happen until Jesus Christ returns.

Such a view is right, but it is also wrong.

It is true that such things will not be universally practiced upon the earth until Jesus Christ physically returns to rule and reign over the entire earth. But this does not mean that we, as representatives of Jesus on earth, cannot begin to practice equality, mercy, freedom, and justice right now.

We must not wait for governments to enact the change, or presidents and congressman to make laws about it, or bank presidents and company CEOs to suddenly change course. If we wait for that, we will truly be waiting until return of Christ. No, we must get out there and put into practice NOW the things we long for, wait for, look for, and hope for.

We must be Jesus to the world.

YOU AND I ARE JESUS TO THE WORLD

We are Jesus Christ to the world, the Body of Christ that is physically present on earth, being the hands and feet and voice of Jesus to a world that is without light and without hope.

So this Christmas season, as we remember the first coming of Jesus Christ, and as we look forward to His Second Coming, also remember to look for ways on how Jesus Christ can return today, in and through you, to someone who needs His touch and His voice in their lives today.

Until the day Jesus returns, He returns today in you.

Jeremy blogs at TillHeComes.org *and is the author of numerous books, including* Put Service Back into the Church Service *and* Church is More than Bodies, Bucks, and Bricks. *He lives in Oregon with his wife and three daughters.*

Photo by Sean Vivek Crasto. Public domain

ELEVENTH DAY OF CHRISTMAS.
January 4. It Begins at Home. *Andy Wade*

11

Recently I posted a somewhat cynical comment on Facebook regarding an event in the news, expressing some frustration. In response, a friend asked the question, "How do we effect change among____ Heck, how do I effect MORE change in myself?" Those questions stirred within me as I wrote a more cool-headed, thoughtful reply. They continue to stir in me precisely because they are essential questions for those of us who follow Christ and take his call to discipleship seriously.

Here's how I responded [*clarifications and further reflections are bracketed*]:

-----I think you touch on two of the most important aspects of change: education and attitude. [*My friend's remarks were more detailed than this*] I'm in a love-hate relationship with Facebook; it's great for getting in touch, and staying in touch, with friends, new and old, but it also is filled with bumper sticker-type proclamations that tend to feed extreme views and fuel anger and cynicism. I admit, I'm part of the problem and have quit reading many of the inflammatory articles and memes that appear (although I was rather cynical in my remarks [*to the article posted on Facebook*] above).

I'm attempting a change in myself for the coming year: If a post gets me angry, I'm trying to force myself to peer underneath my emotions and ask, "Why?" Am I falling into an intentional trap laid out to tick me off? Or is this a legitimate issue to be upset about? If it's legit, how can I better respond in a way that educates, rather than alienates?

My role, as a follower of Jesus, is to be an "ambassador of reconciliation." Too often, I'm an ambassador of discord as I allow myself to be manipulated by media and provocation.

In other words, to effect change requires change first in me. I'm convinced this is the beginning step in personal, spiritual, and social change—and it's not a one-off event, but an ongoing awareness of my internal attitudes, emotions, motivations, and underlying assumptions.

Once I acknowledge this, and begin to put it into practice, I'm (more) ready to begin engaging in healthy spiritual practices which can further shape my inner character. *[One might argue that our first spiritual practice should be to come before God with this kind of open, confessional-repentant attitude.]*

I've come to realize how various "spiritual practices" can easily become just an extension of our broken and often cynical nature if we do not begin with the foundational (and ongoing) process of personal examination. Without this ongoing examination, I put up roadblocks to the work of the Spirit in my life and cripple not only my own spiritual growth, but also my ability to walk effectively alongside others.

With the right attitude engaged, I'm ready to begin to look again at how best to be an agent of change that does not also intentionally or unintentionally alienate many of the people I'm trying to reach. It now becomes more possible for me to become an agent of education and change because I've begun to allow God to shape my heart and mind around not only God's purposes, but God's methods of healing and reconciliation in the world.

What I used to call "education" may well now be revealed to be rather "instigation" and be easily discarded as unhelpful.

Well, those are nice words and thoughts…now to live into them! This is my personal challenge as I enter the new year. Believe it or not, I have been trying to change, but the combination of passion about various extremely important issues and the accessibility (especially through Facebook) of radicalized "news" articles and memes, make it a real challenge to maintain a clear and open attitude. Enter community—good and trustworthy friends who can help hold me (us) accountable to our deeper calling.-----

As I now read back over these words, I'm stunned by both the simplicity and the complexity of my undertaking. The actions themselves are quite simple, the complexity is where emotions and habit enter in. To move forward I must be intentional about all my interactions, especially those that take place online.

Why "especially online?" A few years ago, while talking with a friend, I made the analogy of Facebook posts being like driving on the freeway. Because of the imagined anonymity or distance, people become more aggressive, acting in ways they never would in a face-to-face encounter. What I failed to realize at the time was how much I was also referring to my own online presence!

It Begins at Home.

As I enter this new year, I am challenged by Jesus' very simple, yet complex, invitation: "Come, follow me." This is an invitation to discipleship, and discipleship requires a desire to change. My friend's question, "How do we effect change in [others]?" cannot really be answered until we honestly begin to answer his second question, "How do I effect MORE change in myself?" It begins at home, in our hearts and minds as we truly open our lives—our motivations, assumptions, preconceived notions, prejudices, and attitudes.

Or as Jesus once put it:

"Why do you look at the speck of sawdust in your brother's eye and pay no attention to the plank in your own eye? How can you say to your brother, 'Let me take the speck out of your eye,' when all the time there is a plank in your own eye? You hypocrite, first take the plank out of your own eye, and then you will see clearly to remove the speck from your brother's eye." (Mt. 7:3-5)

Sure, Jesus is talking about passing judgment here, but isn't that precisely where our attitudes often go astray? What, after all, causes me to respond to those I might disagree with by posting a meme that belittles their view (whether it's "right" or "wrong")? Is the root of that motivation not so much in helping the other but rather in my judgment of them?

So returning to my friend's question, paraphrasing it to fit into the real issue I'm facing as a follower of Jesus: "Why do you say to your brother or sister, 'Let me disciple you,' when all along you refuse to be fully discipled by the one who is the true teacher? You hypocrite, first become a true disciple, and then you will have a portion of the humility necessary to help disciple your brother or sister."

Now the difficult work begins.

Andy is a team member of Mustard Seed Associates and is an ordained Mennonite Pastor who has ministered in Seattle and Hong Kong and now lives with his family in Hood River, Oregon. When not working on MSA projects, Andy can be found working in the family's organic garden, hunting wild mushrooms, taking pictures, coordinating volunteers for the Hood River Warming Shelter, or just relaxing in the beauty of the Columbia River Gorge.

TWELFTH DAY OF CHRISTMAS.
January 5. *Gather, Feast, Create*

12

Gather

Twelfth Night is the celebration ending the twelve days of Christmas. Some church communities have a pageant of the arrival of the Magi at Jesus' nativity. Other groups have a big dinner that ends with eating "king cake," a sweet, braided loaf of bread or any cake that has a trinket (sometimes a small plastic baby that traditionally represents Jesus) placed inside or underneath. The eater of the slice of cake containing the trinket is said to have good luck. This gathering also marks the beginning of Epiphany or "Ordinary Time," depending on one's tradition. As you gather this evening, discuss your experience of the twelve days of Christmas, what you would leave out or add next Christmas, and wonder together about epiphanies that you hope to have in the coming weeks.

Feast

Meal: Casserole potluck and king cake

Get creative and bring a favorite casserole or search the Internet and try a new one at your meal tonight. End the evening by eating king cake, baked at home or store-bought. Don't forget to add the trinket!

Create

Twelfth Night is a good time to bless your home for the new year. Chalk blessings are a traditional way to observe this practice, as marks representing the Magi and the New Year are placed on the lintel of the front door. Prayers and blessings may vary. A thoughtful version of this liturgy from New Zealand may be found at http://liturgy.co.nz/epiphany-chalk-house-blessing-2.

—Kristin

O SAPIENTIA

"O Wisdom, O holy Word of God, you govern all creation with your strong yet tender care. Come and show your people the way to salvation."

Epiphany

[Image: Arizona retirement community]

O Wisdom

"Epiphany" is such a mysterious word. It is alternately a singular word used to describe the "manifestation" of Christ to the Magi, the calendar date of January 6, the appearance of a deity, or a quirky concept of sudden discovery. My favorite definition is "a sudden, intuitive perception of or insight into the reality or essential meaning of something, usually initiated by some simple, homely, or commonplace occurrence or experience."[37] I picture a cartoon figure walking along, shoulders slightly hunched, feet dragging, then stopping suddenly and bolting upright as he suddenly "gets it." A light bulb appears in the cartoon bubble over his head, and now he is exuberant, smiling, and striding boldly ahead with his imaginary day.

The signs, symbols, and stories of Epiphany offer us a season between the Magi's arrival at Jesus' nativity and Fat Tuesday to be open to discovery and insight. One year, I endeavored to notice daily epiphanies during these weeks, and I wasn't disappointed. Indeed, these epiphanies were often mundane, such as the brilliant stroke of inspiration that came to me while pushing a heavy double stroller filled with my children through our neighborhood. Sweaty and out of breath, I suddenly decided to rearrange the day of the week I usually did the laundry, so I might have *one more* precious hour of writing time. On another day, I realized that I could actually "friend" a few people on Facebook that I had lost touch with and been reticent to contact. The insights gained were life-giving.

Twelfth Night parties held in our communities give us the opportunity to celebrate the end of the twelve days of Christmas; kings may come dressed in robes bearing casseroles of exotic flavors, evergreen boughs used for decoration may be burned to represent the passing of time. Crowns, flames, and feasting are a tangible reminder that though Christmas has just ended, our journey continues. During Epiphany we encounter Martin Luther King, Jr.'s, birthday, the feast days of St. Brigid, St. Frances de Sales, St. Caedmon, and St. Valentine. All of these saints illumine our paths toward the deeply contemplative season of Lent that will follow. On the last Sunday after the Epiphany, we go with Jesus to the Mount of the Transfiguration and risk standing as Peter, James, and John did in the blinding, sculpting presence of God.

Epiphany is a time of beseeching Wisdom to "show us the way to salvation," to walk with open minds and hearts through the winter days and nights always

---

[37] http://dictionary.reference.com/browse/epiphany

expectant and ever hopeful that with God's "strong but tender care," we will arrive at the beginning of Lent ready to approach that season with clarity and curiosity.

—Kristin

Morning Prayer for the Season of Epiphany

Arise, shine, inheritors of God's light,

bearers of God's light to our darkened world.

The light of God has come into our world,

and nations will come to its brightness.

Arise, shine, privileged ones who live in the light of Christ.

Bow before God, not in shame but in awe.

All is visible in Christ's eternal light.

In us God's light never goes out.

(Pause to remind yourself of the ways that Christ has been revealed as Son of God in your own life. How has God used your life to bring Christ's light into the life of others?)

Arise, shine, in Christ, God's light has been revealed to us.

It reaches across time and space.

We have come to see.

We have come to follow.

Arise, shine, in Christ, God's light has been revealed to all people.

God's glory has been unveiled in all the earth.

May we go and tell.

May we go and share God's light with our needy world.

Come and see.

The light of God has come into our world

to proclaim God's justice and love.

It has overcome the darkness and brought new life.

Come and follow.

Christ our king has redeemed our world.

He draws us into a loving family

from every tribe and family and culture.

Go and tell.

The Spirit has equipped us for service

to love our neighbours as we do ourselves,

to bring God's salvation to the ends of the earth.

Come and see, come and follow, go and tell.

In God's Son, the nations of the earth will put their hope.

Our Father who art in heaven, hallowed be your name, Your kingdom come, your will be done, on earth as it is in heaven. Give us this day our daily bread, and forgive us our trespasses as we forgive those who trespass against us And lead us not into temptation, but deliver us from evil, for yours is the kingdom, the power and the glory, forever and ever, amen

God who revealed yourself to wise men following a star,

guide all who search and journey towards your light today.

God whose light shines like a bright guiding star have mercy on us.

---

[38] www.lectionarypage.net

God who unveiled yourself in the gift of a son,

show yourself to all who seek after justice and righteousness today.

God whose light shines like a bright guiding star have mercy on us.

God who was baptized with those who declared repentance in the Jordan River,

manifest yourself to all who come with repentant hearts today.

God whose light shines like a bright guiding star have mercy on us.

God who fed the five thousand with a handful of fish and loaves,

satisfy our hunger with your word of truth and love.

God whose light shines like a bright guiding star have mercy on us.

God who changed water into wine at a wedding,

fill all who thirst with the free gift of the water of life.

God whose light shines like a bright guiding star have mercy on us.

(Pause to offer up your own intercessions.)

Lord God Almighty, thank you that Jesus' epiphany as Son of God reaches across time and space. As we go into this day may we embrace your call to come and see, come and follow, go and tell. May we remember that we are bearers of Christ's light sent out to touch others, so that they may know him as Son of God and experience the wonderful hope his message brings.

Go into the world knowing you are led by the light of Christ.

May the love of the Creator go before you.

May the life of the Redeemer be within you.

May the joy of the Spirit shine through you.

Amen.

—Christine

EPIPHANY,. January 6. Wise Traditions. *Christi Mitchell*

Epiphany is defined by the Oxford English Dictionary as "the manifestation of Christ to the Gentiles as represented by the Magi (Matthew 2:1-12)." Other meanings include "the festival commemorating the Epiphany on January 6" and "a moment of sudden revelation or insight." Having grown up in a Protestant tradition that did not acknowledge many of the liturgical holidays or feast days, I was only familiar with the last definition until a handful of years ago.

Life changes when you have children. As new parents, my husband and I were eager to establish holiday traditions for our little family. We found ourselves in a church celebrating Advent, and we joined in and learned. Advent, Epiphany, Ash Wednesday, Lent…this was so much more than just Christmas and Easter! We delved deeper. And we fell in love with these new ways to worship and to acknowledge. How had we lived so many years with a stripped-down worship experience? How did we not know that each event on the liturgical calendar was a beautiful celebration of another aspect of the mystery of the Incarnation?

We embraced it all. We found (and still find) so much meaning in the observations of these days. Advent is a season of wonder and mystery and excitement and anticipation, and even though Jesus arrived in our world over 2000 years ago, we still prepare our hearts and our homes for His coming. Every single year we do this, and each year brings the same breathless awe at the mystery of His manifestation. This is our story, and it never grows old.

Every December we find ourselves slowing down, taking time for nightly devotionals as we fill our Jesse Tree. Each morning we find a new reminder of the reason for the season as we open the doors of our Advent calendar. But these traditions END on Christmas Day, and the birth of Christ was not the end. It's a midpoint, rather, the fulfilling of the prophecies of the Old Testament and the beginning of the healing of our broken relationship with the Father. There was all that came before, and then the birth, and then all that came after.

Christmas Day is not the end of the season. And though it ends the twelve days of Christmas, neither is the Epiphany. I think the significance of the Epiphany has been lost to many. It's the day we take the Christmas decorations down or the day we add the Wise Men to our nativity scenes. It's the day we eat the first king cake of the season. But it's so much more than that. It's a celebration of the incarnation of Jesus, of his first appearance to the Gentiles. Here was a Savior for all the people. ALL the people. We don't end our reveling here and just take a break in our cleaned and undecorated homes until Ash Wednesday arrives. We have much more to praise, so much more to remember. Let's take the time to acknowledge His life before we begin the observance of His death and resurrection. In just a few short years, this man, this Son of God, changed the course of our destiny, of our eternity. Not just with His birth or with His death, but with His life and His teachings and His healings and His enduring message of love. The momentum of the Advent season, the joy of His glorious arrival—it continues well past the Feast of the Epiphany. Keep it going forward—don't stop celebrating; don't give those post-holiday blues a chance. We have much to celebrate—too much to confine to just one short season!

Christi Mitchell lives in central Alabama with her husband, son, three dogs, and two Guinea pigs and is sadly the only female in the bunch. She delightedly embraces small town life and loves working as a full time Children's Minister, full-time wife, and full-time mom.

DR. MARTIN LUTHER KING, JR.'S, BIRTHDAY. January 15. MLK: The Man, the Icon, the Saint. *Jodi Baron*

For my whole life, all 37 years of it, I have read and heard stories about Martin Luther King., Jr.[39] As a college student, studying race and gender issues, his work was most definitely present in my studies.

However, it was as I began to live into my role as parent when his words began to take root. To imagine a world where my children might judge others not by the color of their skin but by the content of their heart, the beloved community our faith as Christ-followers invites each of us to not only imagine but be cocreators of.

Well, as one might expect, conversations in my home with my three elementary-school-aged daughters regarding race have been more frequent lately with the events dominating our news headlines, of terrible racial hatred and violence in the U.S.

But their questions are familiar ones to me. As a white girl growing up in a small town in midwestern America, race wasn't something that got brought up in my daily conversations. So when injustice did happen it was all the more disruptive for our community.

---

[39] Editor's Note: Martin Luther King, Jr., Day celebrates Dr. King's birthday and is observed on the third Monday in January in the United States.

To think that someone we kids interacted with daily, respected highly, and loved dearly was being treated differently because the color of his skin was darker than the majority of our community, hurt me more deeply than I could have thought possible.

But, as sensitive as I am to the injustices captivating our national imagination, I am attentive to the fact that I do not, nor will I ever be able to fully, grasp how deep and painful and pervasive this issue affects my brothers and sisters of African descent.

Nevertheless, I continue to try.

I continue to share the stories of Martin Luther King, Jr., and of my childhood, and to listen to the stories and to talk about the questions my daughters have.

A few years ago, the local university was holding their annual MLK peace march. My middle daughter was in pre-school at the time and was learning about MLK in her classroom. She expressed interest in participating in the march. So we put on our shoes and walked over to the rallying place, a green space in the center of the campus. Organizers had booths set up for people to be able to make signs. They had pieces of paper with quotes from Dr. King. My daughter leafed through the quotes, and asked me to read them to her. When she discovered the one that spoke to her the most, I sat the paper in front of her and she began to copy the letters onto her poster board. And then we walked. We marched with the thousands of people that day remembering Dr. King, celebrating the accomplishments we've had in the years since his assassination, and recognizing the work yet to be done. It was a moment of cultural healing and of teaching my children.

I think the key to addressing racial issues in our country, especially with our children, isn't to shy away from the conversations and questions they have, but to engage them. More than ever, we in the U.S. recognize cultural differences and I think that's something to rejoice. We all have things to share, and if we are patient and practice listening, we may even hear healing take place, one relationship at a time.

Jodi is an ordained minister in the Episcopal Church serving Grace Episcopal Church in Holland, Michigan. She and her husband have been married for 14 years and have three children.

PETER'S CONFESSION. January 18.
Are We Christian? *Stephen Crippen*

icon: Peter and Paul

Most days of the week, I go to meetings with friends of mine where we drink coffee and talk in a circle. The meetings open and close with prayer, but they're not religious services like this one. They're informal, and they are not even Christian, or allied with any religious tradition. We share what's been going on in our lives, and we encourage newcomers to follow our spiritual path.

Whenever I speak in this meeting, I follow the simple protocol we have in place: I introduce myself by my first name, and I make a very short identity statement, something particular about myself, about who I am.

I say this: "Hi, I'm Stephen, I'm an alcoholic."

That's the basic formula.

I don't say, "Hi, I'm Stephen, I'm a deacon;" or, "I'm a psychotherapist;" or a brother, spouse, uncle, friend, son, godfather, baptized Christian… Of course I *am* all of those things. But the group doesn't need to hear my insights as a therapist, or wisdom I've gained as a godfather. They need to hear what I've learned about myself, and my mistakes, and my gratitude, through the lens of my identity as an alcoholic. I begin with that identity; everything flows from that.

Some in the group like to put a little creative spin on the formula, which I find interesting. They might say, "Hi, I'm Stephen, I'm sober today," emphasizing the fact that anyone in recovery has only these 24 hours: today is the only day we need to worry about. Others might say, "Hi, I'm Stephen, I'm sober, but still sick," acknowledging the reality that we are never done with our spiritual work; we are always in need of healing. Still others might say, "Hi, I'm Stephen, I'm a grateful, recovering alcoholic," expressing our identity in a positive way, celebrating the powerful gratitude we feel for one another, our higher power, and the grace and peace that surrounds us now.

But I don't do a creative spin, in part because in my drinking days I did a lot of creative spinning. I like to follow the traditional formula. Speaking only for myself, it's much safer this way.

Identity shapes what we say or do next. Identity sends us in a certain direction. If we identify ourselves as someone or something, be careful: what happens next?

"Who do people say that the Son of Man is[40]?" Jesus asks his friends. An identity question. When we hear it, we can easily assume that he is just being clever: he knows who he is, right? So it must be a kind of trick question, a setup: he's just preparing his friends for a dramatic revelation of his true identity. But that's not the case, not in that place and time. Biblical scholars sometimes call the people of the ancient Mediterranean "dyadic personalities[41]," that is, they were not entirely self-defined like we tend to be in our own era. You and I live in a world of distinct, unique individuals. We get to say for ourselves who we are and who we are not. But in the time and place of Jesus, one's identity was "dyadic," two-fold, a combination of my own self-conscious awareness of who I am alongside the opinions of everybody else. "Who do people say that the Son of Man is?"—this is a *dyadic* question. Jesus wants to know the other side of his identity, the side that is given to him by those who know him.

And his friends know the answer. They can hear what people are saying about Jesus. John the Baptist, Elijah, Jeremiah, one of the prophets: he could easily accept the respectable identity given to him by others—the voice of God proclaiming justice in his own time, a prophet who says and does things the way other famous prophets have always done.

Except he doesn't stop there.

"But who do *you* say that I am?" he then asks his friends. He pushes the envelope. What does his inner circle think? They've been around him the most. They've been there as he opened the eyes of the blind: not just a wondrous act of healing, but a powerful sign of spiritual enlightenment. This Jesus was up to something special. So...who is he? *He* wanted to know. He couldn't define himself alone; he needed his friends' assessment.

---

[40] The readings for the week Stephen preached this sermon in the summer of 2014 were: Isaiah 51:1-6, Psalm 138, Romans 12:1-8, and Matthew 16:13-20. With his permission, his sermon has been reprinted here for use on the day set aside to remember St. Peter's confession that Jesus was the Messiah.

[41] John Pilch, *The Cultural World of Jesus, Sunday by Sunday, Year A* (Collegeville, MN: The Liturgical Press, 1995)

And Simon Peter obliges: he moves beyond the conventional wisdom about Jesus and calls him "Messiah," the anointed one, the one who was promised.

And it is here that I feel a little worried about Peter. I wonder if he understands what he's saying, and more importantly if he understands what he might have to endure in light of what he's saying. If he's following the Messiah and not just a prophet, what might that mean for Peter himself, and his companions? If Jesus is the Messiah, then Peter won't be able to simply go back to his old life if the movement dies out.

If Jesus is the Messiah, the movement *can't* die out.

And sure enough, Peter is praised warmly by Jesus for confessing him to be the Messiah, and immediately given a central role in the community, complete with a new name: Rock. Simon is now Rock, the foundation stone of a movement that's much bigger than him, much bigger than this band of friends, much bigger and daunting and dangerous than anything this little group imagined when they first said Yes to the invitation to follow their leader.

And so Jesus, well aware of how dangerous it can be for his friends to start telling their neighbors that they've found the Messiah, puts a damper on things by "sternly" ordering them not to talk about it. One step at a time, he seems to be saying. But the time soon comes when Peter and all the others take the message throughout the countryside, and even across the sea. And the time soon comes when they lose their lives for proclaiming the Good News. The Gospel upends everything: to follow Jesus and claim him as Messiah is Good News for the poor and the oppressed. And that can be *bad* news for those who disturb the peace in this way. If everyone—rich and poor, powerful and weak, insider and outsider—if everyone simply holds still and doesn't cause any trouble, then no one gets hurt. But that's not a luxury Rock and his friends can enjoy, if they want to follow the Messiah. They must claim his identity themselves; they must step into the fray.

And so they do.

Can you see how dangerous it is to claim an identity?

In our own place and time, alcoholics like me have something in common with Peter and his friends: we enjoy the protection of anonymity. As long as they didn't talk openly about Jesus as Messiah, they had time to prepare themselves for what was coming. And as long as I stay silent about my alcoholism, I can avoid the awkwardness and embarrassment of people knowing my whole story.

Decades ago, it was even worse for alcoholics, and the anonymity was not about shame as much as self-preservation: anonymity creates a necessary safe zone. (It can also foster a helpful humility, which is something I usually lack: recovery is not about displaying one's accomplishments for all to see.)

But at some point, it's time to come out. It's time for Rock and his friends to state openly who they are, who they follow, and what that means. Even if they pay with their lives.

Most of the people gathered here claim the identity of "Christian," a follower of Christ. We would do well to understand how serious this is. If we are Christians, and if we confess that publicly, then some daunting, even disturbing things flow from that identity.

If we are Christian, then we cannot stand by and be neutral when Ferguson, Missouri, erupts in racial violence. We have to stand up for the black boys who were gunned down, and also interact prophetically—and pastorally—with the cops and Ferguson residents who are caught up in this crisis.

If we are Christian, then we cannot stand by and be neutral when this planet groans with the upheaval of climate change. We have to confront our own complicity in uncontrolled carbon emissions, our own easy tolerance of animal cruelty, our own dependence on an agricultural and industrial infrastructure that is damaging the earth God proclaimed good.

If we are Christian, then we cannot stand by and be neutral when the church itself harms its own people with intolerance, rejection, or abuse.

If we are Christian… there is no end to the implications of this identity statement.

Are we Christian?

Are we sure we want to be?

Who do *you* say that we are?

Stephen Crippen is a deacon in the Episcopal Church serving at St. Paul's in Seattle and also works in a private practice as a psychotherapist, primarily with couples.

FEAST OF ST. FRANCES DE SALES. January 24. The Light Increases. *Hailey Spencer*

Every December, I find myself staying closer to home as the days grow shorter.[42] When it's dark by the time I get done with school I never really feel as though it's daytime. By Christmas, I'm good and sick of it, and it's a relief to watch the paper for the sunrise and sunset times and the light increases. Each progressively later sunset becomes a small celebration, so maybe it's not surprising that this time of increasing daylight coincides with Epiphany.

January is a strange time of year. The increase of daylight means nothing to the weather outside, which for those of us in Seattle means it's rainy and cold. The constant gray makes it easy to feel as though nothing is happening or changing. It starts as a whisper. Two more minutes of daylight. It doesn't seem like anything noteworthy until it starts to accumulate. Two more, and then two more, and finally, the day when school is finished but the sun is still there, holding on for a few more minutes, and suddenly, it's not a whisper anymore, and something new has manifested.

When I think of Easter, another important time in the church year, I think of noise, and rejoicing. I think of the word "Hallelujah!" repeated at every opportunity. When I think of Epiphany, it takes a few minutes before anything comes to the surface, but if I'm still and pay enough attention, things begin to emerge. It's a renewal of light and hope after the darkest part of the year. The time when nothing seems to happen, but everything manages to change before our eyes.

Thinking about this always makes me wonder about my own life, how the days and weeks have added up until suddenly, I'm different than I was a year ago. I can never pinpoint what caused it, but when I'm feeling low in the winter, I remind myself about the gift of two extra minutes.

Moving away for college was a challenge; progress couldn't be measured in increments of time. I had to find new ways to count growth, new ways to remind myself that just because change can be quiet doesn't mean it's not there. Now, I count meals cooked by myself and papers turned in on time. I count the

---

[42]Editor's note: St Frances de Sales (1567-1622) is known in the Roman Catholic Church as the patron saint for writers and journalists. I chose to include Hailey's piece on this day to honor her craft of writing.

times I've made myself stop and think about the best ways to take care of myself. Pulling open my blinds in the morning or getting a good night's sleep feel like singular gestures rather than growth, but just like the minutes of daylight, I find myself making a quiet transformation.

In the depths of winter, the first morning when the sun is up before me always takes me by surprise. No matter how long I've been anticipating it, I still feel as though it's snuck up on me. At first, I might not even notice what's happened, but I can feel in my body that something's different. And suddenly, I've made it through another winter, two minutes of daylight at a time.

Hailey Spencer is a writing student who splits her time between Seattle and the San Francisco Bay Area. She enjoys camping in the Pacific Northwest, reading, and her continuous attempts to beat her dad at chess. She can often be found lurking in coffee shops or scribbling poetry at a bus stop. She is currently enrolled at Mills College and working towards her B.A. in English.

FEAST OF ST. BRIGID. February 1.
Brigid. *Mary Keenan*

Brigid—known also as Brigit, Bridget, Brid, Bride—is a patroness of Ireland, along with Patrick and Columba. Her life mirrors a huge cultural shift during the 5th and 6th Centuries, when Christianity was introduced to the pagan clans of Medieval Ireland.

There is a tale in which Brigid is asked by friends to visit a dying pagan chieftain. He was delirious in his illness and they hoped she could calm. As she sat by his bedside, she picked up some rushes from the floor (common in those days to keep the room warm and clean) and started weaving them together into the shape of a cross. As she wove, she explained the meaning of the cross to the sick man, who grew quiet and listened. Soon his fever broke. The story of love she told him, the Christian story, so captivated the chieftain, that he was baptized just before his death.

Brigid's cross of rushes gently bent her natural surroundings into the shape of her faith—just as Brigid wove the people and culture of Ireland into a Christian  people. Born to a pagan chieftain father and a Christian slave mother, Brigid's family included the two communities that she bridged through her life and work, teaching pagan Ireland how to embrace a new faith, while keeping its unique cultural character.

Christianity came to Ireland, not through political power, but through individual acts of faith and storytelling by people on the underside of history. Born a slave, Brigid spent her life helping the poor. Many of the miracles attributed to her are tales of feeding the hungry, giving away worldly goods, and being mysteriously rewarded for her generosity. When, as a child, she gave away all her mother's butter, it was replenished threefold. She kept a secret store of clothes and food for the poor and in one story, even gave her father's treasured sword to a leper.

Brigid showed how her Christian faith incorporated elements that were valued among her pagan neighbors—respect for the natural world and strong bonds of kinship. She is most notable for forming religious communities that became centers of prayer, charity and learning for both women and men. It was from these tight-knit communities that early Irish Christians reached out to the rest of Ireland.

The following prayer is attributed to St. Brigid and sums up the earthy, joyful, communal faith she shared:

I'd like to give a lake of beer to God.
I'd love the heavenly
Host to be tippling there
For all eternity.

I'd love the men of Heaven to live with me,
To dance and sing.
If they wanted, I'd put at their disposal
Vats of suffering.

White cups of love I'd give them
With a heart and a half;
Sweet pitchers of mercy I'd offer
To every man.

I'd make Heaven a cheerful spot
Because the happy heart is true.
I'd make the men contented for their own sake.
I'd like Jesus to love me too.

I'd like the people of heaven to gather
From all the parishes around.
I'd give a special welcome to the women,
The three Marys of great renown

I'd sit with the men, the women and God
There by the lake of beer.
We'd be drinking good health forever
And every drop would be a prayer.

Mary Keenan lives in Austin, Texas, with two kids, a husband, and a dog. She has an M.Div. From Yale Divinity School and loves to think theologically about almost everything. She also loves metaphors, tangents, and rabbit trails and where they lead. Among her thousands of jobs she is a teacher, preacher, strategic planner, grant writer, fundraiser, and writer. She blogs at maryology.com.

CANDLEMAS. The Presentation of Jesus at the Temple. February 2. The Missing Christmas Characters.
Gary Heard.

During the Christmas season, we watched and enjoyed many Christmas pageants and presentations, awash with adapted tea towels, dressing gowns and other household items deployed in adorning various Christmas characters, much to the delight of parents and families, along with members of faith communities.[43] Children (and older folk!) from all walks of life donned apparel in order to depict the story of Mary and Joseph, and the birth of Jesus. Angels, shepherds, Magi, along with various animals, all served to elaborate the scene which is depicted on Christmas cards and echoed in the familiar carols which permeate so many public spaces in that season.

But two people who are an integral part of this story never appear. There are no carols mentioning their names. They are not memorialised on Christmas cards, and no children will be invited to represent their part in the pageant. They are not considered part of the magic of Christmas, though their presence in the story points to an important and fundamental aspect of faith and service.

Simeon and Anna were elderly citizens, who for years had frequented the temple, praying for their people Israel, in the hope that the promised Messiah would appear. In their advanced years, they held on to a hope which had been met only with silence from the heavens for four centuries. And they have an important role in the Christmas story long before the Magi arrive on the scene.

---

[43] Editor's Note: Candlemas is the Christian holiday remembering Jesus' presentation at the Temple and is celebrated in many ways and given various names in other cultures, including St. Brigid's Day, Imbolc, and Groundhog's Day. It is a day that celebrates the gradual return of light—the hope of sowing a new crop, hearing birds beginning to sing, noticing buds on plants. In some church traditions, candles are brought to be blessed by a pastor for the year to come. More information may be found at www.schooloftheseasons.com/html.

They take their place in the story on the eighth day—the day of Jesus'
presentation in the temple. The sight of Jesus, for them, marks the culmination
of a long journey of prayer and hope. They greet Jesus with a blessing, with his
parents.

For all their yearning and the place they have to pronounce a blessing on Jesus,
their moment is fleeting. When Jesus and his family depart the temple that day,
Simeon and Anna fade into the background. They would not live to see the
fulfillment of the very things they hoped for and declared. They demanded no
further involvement in Jesus' life, and presumably returned to their humble
prayers, fuelled in hope by the reality of having seen Jesus. They let go, leaving
what followed in the hands of God—and others.

When we have invested so much of ourselves in a particular hope, it can be
difficult to let go and trust that the outcome does not depend on our continued
involvement. Simeon and Anna remind us that our purpose is not primarily to
make a better world for ourselves, nor to ensure that every rich opportunity
blesses us. The faith they demonstrate is a gift to those who follow after them.

That they do not appear in Christmas celebrations reminds us that important
aspects of the Christmas story are easily forgotten, particularly in our family-
oriented celebrations. The message that God is born in the midst of our chaotic
and broken world, into the war-torn and ravaged places of life—is the key
Christmas message for us to remember. God IS with us, even—perhaps
especially—in the darkest moments of life.

*Gary Heard is pastor of an inner-city Baptist church in Melbourne, and now shares this role
as Dean of Whitley College—the Baptist theological college in Melbourne. He is married to
Evelyn and they have three children. Gary and Evelyn have a long relationship with Mustard
Seed Associates.*

Song of Simeon

Lord, you now have set your servant free
to go in peace as you have promised;

For these eyes of mine have seen the Savior,
whom you have prepared for all the world to see:

A Light to enlighten the nations,
and the glory of your people Israel.

Glory to the Father, and to the Son, and to the Holy Spirit:
as it was in the beginning, is now, and will be for ever. Amen.

(Book of Common Prayer, 135)
Based on Luke 2: 29-32

FEAST OF ST. CAEDMON. February 11. Song of Ourselves. *Erin Jean Warde*

The story of St. Caedmon's is one of my favorites, because it is the story of a man who was given a talent from God. We know about his story, because it was written by the Venerable Bede. The story goes that in the middle of the seventh century when Caedmon, the keeper of the animals, was with the people of the monastery, one night a harp was passed from person to person, so that they could sing their poetry to the tune of the harp. Before the harp could get to him, Caedmon left the group out of shame, because he did not have any poetry to offer, and was unable to sing. He left his friends and went to sleep, in sadness.

In his dreams, he had a vision of someone calling him by name, and calling him to sing. He explained that he could not. The vision asked again, asking him to sing about creation. Suddenly, Caedmon began to sing! He sang verses praising God for the many gifts of creation. These verses would later be known as "Caedmon's Hymn," but at the time they were only known to him. He told his friends in the monastery about his vision, and sang to them his hymn. The community believed that this gift of singing was given to him by God, as a blessing.

I knew the story of Caedmon in passing before I went to seminary, but it was first made incarnate for me while in Austin, Texas, at Seminary of the Southwest. My friends, Kristin and Michael, have a son named Caedmon, and as a community, we were invited to celebrate his feast day by sharing our artistic talents. It was a beautiful mixture of faces and gifts, all of which I could recognize as being divinely offered, just like St. Caedmon's. The story of St. Caedmon takes on new form when you can see gifts given to people that you know, and gifts offered in worship.

When I left seminary, I moved to Waco, Texas, to work at St. Paul's Episcopal Church. I was given the task of looking critically and creatively at how we do ministry as a community, meaning how we welcome new people, have fun events for people of all ages, and how we connect our fun time together with our spiritual growth. I put on a St. Caedmon's Open Mic Night, which is a time that we invite anyone from the congregation to come forward and share a gift they've been given by God. I start the night by sharing the story of St. Caedmon, then invite people of all ages to share their gifts. We gather in just the candlelight of our chapel, and the stage is set for us to sit in wonder at the many ways that God blesses God's people. From silly magician routines, to heartfelt poetry, to camp songs on the six-string, we have done this event two years in a row, and it is a magical space in time for me.

I love the connection that the story of St. Caedmon makes between our gifts and our God, our passions and our piety. The story of St. Caedmon helps us connect our gifts to the greater story of Christ, because we can see how God is actively working in the world today. When we see God's work in the world as connected to our talents, we can see Christ as not only coming into the world to heal and to bring life into the world, but also to bring into the world the sort of laughter and joy that leads us into abundant life.

The Rev. Erin Jean Warde is Assistant Rector at St. Paul's Episcopal Church in Waco, Texas, and College Missioner to the Episcopal Student Center in Waco. She received her bachelor's degree in English and Creative Writing from Troy University in Troy, Alabama, and received her Masters of Divinity from Seminary of the Southwest in Austin, Texas.

ST. CAEDMON'S DAY. February 11. *Gather, Feast, Create*

Gather

St. Caedmon, who lived at Whitby Abbey in what is now northeastern England during the abbacy (657-680) of St. Hilda (614-680), is known as the first Anglo-Saxon poet. Some scholars believe the first hymn he wrote, "St. Caedmon's Hymn," is the first example of Old English poetry. This poem is extraordinary

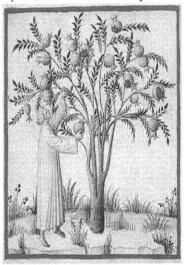

in that Caedmon, the lowly monastery cowherd, received the inspiration to sing it in a dream from God. As Rev. Erin Jean Warde described in her essay for his feast day, gathering to share a feast and your talents is a fun way to honor this lesser-known Christian holiday. At the end of the evening, consider reading Caedmon's poem together. The children's picture book *Caedmon's Song* written by Ruth Ashby and illustrated by Bill Slavin is also an excellent way to share the story.

Feast

Meal: English potluck with ales or teas

In honor of St. Caedmon's Celtic heritage, enjoy a meal of English foods, such as shepherd's pie, trifle, fish n' chips, and a selection of English ales or teas. In the early medieval tradition of sharing songs, stories, and poems over the meal, try playing a dinner game that begins with a story-starter: the host chooses the first line of the story which then continues around the table with each guest adding the next few lines.

Create

After the meal, enjoy an open mic/talent night where guests offer a song, story, or skit and share the story of Caedmon. Enjoy celebrating God's diversity of given talents in community.

—Kristin

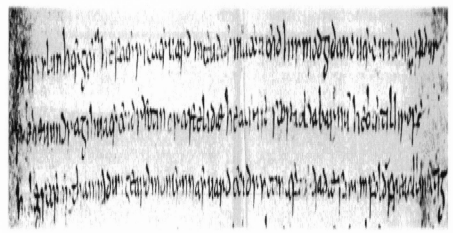

"Caedmon's Hymn," public domain

St. Caedmon's Hymn (Modern English translation)

Now [we] must honour the guardian of heaven,

the might of the architect, and his purpose,

the work of the father of glory

as he, the eternal lord, established the beginning of wonders;

he first created for the children of men

heaven as a roof, the holy creator

Then the guardian of mankind,

the eternal lord, afterwards appointed the middle earth,

the lands for men, the Lord almighty

Old English version:

nu scylun hergan hefaenricaes uard

metudæs maecti end his modgidanc

uerc uuldurfadur swe he uundra gihwaes

eci dryctin or astelidæ

he aerist scop aelda barnum

heben til hrofe haleg scepen.

tha middungeard moncynnæs uard

eci dryctin æfter tiadæ

firum foldu frea allmectig[44]

---

[44] Marsden, Richard, *Old English Reade*, (Cambridge: Cambridge University Press, 2004,) 80, collated with manuscript facsimile.

FEAST OF ST. VALENTINE. February 14.
Gold as Transparent as Glass. *Greg Valerio*

FairTrade gold wedding band, Greg Valerio

Gold is truly a liminal material.[45] It has come to represent the intersection of humanity's most aspirational desires, its most complex social degradations and the most sordid corruptions of the human soul. It is a symbol of our conflicted humanity. In my work over the years as a pioneering ethical jeweller, I have seen the sheer joy on the face of a newly married couple—the gold wedding bands symbolising their love, commitment and fidelity towards one another. Contrast the 15 million artisanal gold miners in Africa alone who will be lucky if they earn $2 a day and will stand (for 12 hours in many cases) up to their waists in mud washing small gold particles, and then amalgamating this with liquid mercury to realise the small dollar value mentioned above.

In the jungles of Colombia, the Afro-Colombian community, the descendants of the slave trade, who were trafficked to work the Conquistador's gold mines, fight for their very cultural integrity against corrupt politicians, illegal miners and pension-fund-supported transnational mining companies, who want their land because they are rich in gold and platinum. This gold rush means the destruction of one of the world's most biodiverse rainforests. And if Colombia is too far away from our daily lives, the toxic legacy of gold mining in the Sierra Nevadas of California means that the Sierra Fund is working to remediate the 19 million pounds of liquid mercury left in the watersheds from the 1849 gold rush. I would not eat the fish in this part of the world, or drink the water. And all because of the corrosive power that the greed for gold can have on the human condition.

---

[45] Editor's note: I've chosen to include Greg's important piece on St. Valentine's Day because of the large amounts of jewelry that are purchased as gifts for this holiday. The "original" Valentine, Valentinus, was martyred in the third century for refusing to deny Christ to the Roman emperor Claudius. Legend has it that while in prison, Valentine gave his testimony and through prayer healed the blind daughter of the jailer. On the day of his execution, lore has it that he sent the daughter a note signed, "Your Valentine."

Illegal Mining in the Congo, Greg Valerio.

So as we come to reflect during this time from Advent to Lent on the hope that is held in the arrival of Divine innocence in human form, the arrival of gold at the cradle of the King, can take on a significance that will perhaps deepen our understanding of how powerful this image truly is. God graces us with his Divine innocence and hails the beginning of creation's homeward journey from the simplicity of His cradle. It is this burden of innocence that we embrace as we enter this season. In my office at home, I have a small box in which I keep gold, frankincense and myrrh - a constant reminder to me of the burden of hope that pure innocence presents to us. Gold a corrupted product is not exempt from this act of redemption.

Over the last 20 years, I have become best known for my work in securing Fairtrade gold to the international jewellery markets. It has become a small but significant contribution to the emancipation of the poor and exploited and has led me to understand the true nature and essence of gold as a created precious metal. In Christ, the Apostles redefined how we as followers of Christ encounter creation. Whether from Eden to the new Adam in Paul, or from the Hebrew exilic polemic of six-day creation in Genesis (written in Babylon) to St. John's opening creational masterpiece,

All things came into being through Him, and without Him not one thing has come into being (Gospel of John 1 v. 3a, New Revised Standard Version, Anglicized Edition).

Gold as a part of God's redemptive plan for creation is as subject to John's vision as every other part of life, whether we are animal, vegetable or mineral. In Christ, we find all of creation bound and caught up in the Godhead and it is therefore appropriate that gold, the agent of such corruption, should be presented to the author of creation at His birth. This very act of laying gold at the feet of Jesus in the cradle by representatives of the Kings of the earth, is paralleled later in John's Apocalyptic vision of the New Jerusalem, where the eternal City is created from '*pure gold, clear as glass*' (Revelation 21 v. 18b, King James Version). Pure gold shall be under the feet of all of the redeemed. A beautiful vision of creation, fall and ultimate redemption.

If we can secure the righteous trading of gold, with full transparency and traceability in the supply chain, we would be delivering gold to the world in the way that God truly intended. This is why we need Fairtrade gold, a gold that benefits the poor, protects the environment, is transparent and traceable from mine to retail and as such is pure and true and a blessing to all.

I finish with a story from Sierra Leone. On a trip to Lake Sonfon, I met the deputy Chief of a Chiefdom who was also a gold miner and trader. Under him, he had approximately 10,000 gold diggers delivering anywhere up to $150,000 USD of gold per week. Every month, American and Ukrainian traders would come to his village and buy his gold. With them, they would bring numerous crates of beer, which would be consumed after the gold deals had been transacted. A girl, around nine years old, came to me, and reaching into her dress pocket opened up a cigarette paper in which was some gold. She told me that this was her main household income. She procured this gold by sitting under the trading table of the deputy chief. She told me once the men started drinking, some for the gold that was being traded would fall off the edge of the table and she would scoop it up in her hands and sell it on at a later date. The gold crumbs from the table. The irony of this story is that whilst American dollars were enriching the elite, the village this girl lived in had no electricity, no running water, no health clinic and no school. This story is repeated thousands of times every day across the gold trade.

As we contemplate Christ and the incarnation of God in human history, may we pray that gold, as transparent as glass may become for us a sign of His

Kingdom, and justice and a means by which the poor may find a way out of charitable donations.

To support righteousness and justice in the gold trade, please buy Fairtrade gold, and ask your local jeweller to stock Fairtrade gold wedding rings.

To find out where you can buy Fairtrade gold jewellery please visit www.fairgold.org

Greg Valerio is a contemplative activist. He is the Founder of The Society of St. Columba and also a participant of Axiom Global Monastic community. He works with the jewellery trade to bring transparency, traceability, righteousness and justice to the trading of gold, diamonds and gemstones. He is married to Ruth Valerio, has two daughters and lives in southern England. To find out more about Greg's work as a campaigner for ethical and fair trade jewellery, please read Making Trouble—Fighting *for* Fairtrade Jewellery *available at* www.valeriobooks.com *or through* Amazon. *Greg regularly blogs at* http://www.chasingcolumba.com.

TRANSFIGURATION SUNDAY.
Transfiguration. *Michael Carroccino*

"Then Peter said to Jesus, 'Rabbi, it is good for us to be here; let us make three dwellings, one for you, one for Moses, and one for Elijah.' He did not know what to say, for they were terrified" (Mark 9:5-6 NRSV).

Is terror the appropriate
response to God?
Absolutely.

For we are surrounded
nowhere to run
in this deep mountain
gorge—the sky shrouded
in mist obscuring the origin
of distant avalanche rumble
and the close (too close?) sharp reports
of boulders breaking free
to plummet alongside
rushing cascades frantic to escape
into the chasm below the pass—the boundary.
Unwilling to join the deadly mad
cacophonous dash to the sea,
there is no destination but up
and—stripped of the option to flee –
ours is the persistent
slow
trudge of great altitude
becoming greater.
a divine summons? a chance gathering of mountaineers?
are they different?
My body knows only
the heightened awareness, the too-quick laughter
and quickened pulse of anticipation

Is terror the appropriate
response to God?
Absolutely.

For this *terra*—not so *firma*—
is unforgiving and steep:
unsteady to the step,
unyielding to the fall,
and uncaring to hope
or ambition.
Cinching boots and hoisting packs
we place our lies in the hands
of that which only faith
(and earthquakes, landslides, avalanche, etc.)
can move.
Is it passion? idle time? image-conscious machismo?
are they different?
my body knows only
the intensifying ache of overloaded joints
the relentless conquer of inertia
and the raw chafing of unfamiliar territory.

Is terror the appropriate
response to God?
Absolutely.

For I left the high pass
traveling alone in the blaze
of midday to higher still
into a cloudless sky
forsaking the roaring gorge
to spend a night exposed
quaking, restless, with labored breath.
Is it terror? the chill of nearby glaciers?
the altitude?
are they different?
My body knows only
the weary discomfort,
the building awareness that I cannot
survive long in this place.

Is terror the appropriate
response to God?
Absolutely.

For as the new day arrives
and the glorious blazing star
tints the clouds with its
beautiful fury, I know without knowing
I am no longer alone (was I ever?)
unaccountably wary, I turn and
just there, a horned shaggy beast
its black eyes fixed on mine, widened
fierceness examines me with intent
measuring my gaze, my stance
my fear
my kinship
before I am deemed a worthy witness
for its rugged hind.
And it is gone.
Is it a divine encounter? a mountain goat?
are they different?
My body knows only
the pricked awareness of being watched
the danger of mystery,
and the enfolding rush
of recognition, deep connection
terror transformed
is transcendent, sublime.

Is terror the appropriate
response to God?
Absolutely.

Michael serves as a priest at St. Mark's Episcopal Cathedral in Seattle. When not creating kitchen chaos in his quest for gastronomic bliss, he enjoys spending time in nature with his wife and two young children. More of his writing may be found in his and Kristin's forthcoming book Boats Without Oars: Ancient-Future Evangelism, An American Road Trip and Collected Stories from the Episcopal Church.

FAT TUESDAY. Mardi Gras. Last Day of Epiphany. Churchly Hunger Games: Carnival into Lent. *Dale Caldwell*

It is late August at Starbucks, and the fruits of the earth are available at the scan of one's smart phone. That's true at all seasons, not just at harvest, at Lammas tide. The pumpkin spice latte is always available now. I am drinking Brazilian coffee and wanting a new toy, a console, so I can play a game that's about to be

released. The game is called *Destiny*, and one of its tag lines is "it doesn't matter who you were; only what you will become." In the game I could save the world. In the game, I could face real danger. In the game, I could become legend. Sitting at Starbucks, the biggest danger is that I will eat too many madeleines and get fat.

It was not always so. There was a time when the calendar was more than twelve pages of paper put together with staples. When there were seasonal food shortages, when knowledge of times and seasons was high tech, the calendar was an interactive game with high stakes. "Eat, drink, and be merry, for tomorrow we may die" was not just an excuse to overindulge. It was a reminder that the feast we have now might be our last. Winter was a time of real danger, when people starved. Spring planting times were fraught with anxiety: the seeds might not come up. There was a struggle, and to participate meant one might succeed and become legend, or one might perish. Not everyone might participate, might interact, all the time. Some are more heroic than others, but we all can support the hero and be willing to take our turn.

On the night before Beowulf battled Grendel, his friends feasted. While he fought, they fasted. On the night before Jesus was handed over to suffering and death, he took bread, and his friends feasted with him. While they were unaware of the outcome, they fasted. It is how they all could interact within the great game of life versus death, and it is how we still can interact in that great game as it is reenacted in the church calendar.

In a world with Brazilian coffee on order in the hinterland of Arkansas, where obesity is a more prevalent problem than hunger, the symbolic value of feast and fast might seem to be obsolete. Carnival and Mardi Gras become entertainments, not participations. Fasting from food is often replaced with "fast from/feast on" lists. But the prevalence of obesity is itself an indication how deep-rooted and powerful our ancient food concerns are. Our genes still wonder whether the feast we have now might be our last.

How can we use the deep-rooted power of the calendar in our fights with the Grendels, the sufferings, the deaths, of our day? To start with, by playing the game, not just watching. Play passionately, as if not less than everything depended upon it. Feast as if tomorrow we may die, because we will surely die. Then fast with bated breath because we really don't know how the struggle will end. There is in the orthodox tradition a wonderful suspension of disbelief during the great three days, which end with people going to the church to see if indeed Jesus does rise. It is not a foregone conclusion.

We live in a time when it is really possible for all people to come to enjoy the fruits of the earth I enjoy at my table at Starbucks in Fayetteville, Arkansas, not just physically in the papaya juice and madeleines and Brazilian coffee, but mentally in the information that is available with a mere question my cell phone that also pays for my coffee, a genie that fulfills far more than three wishes. But it is a time when ignorance and fear strive to tear us apart, to divide us in many ways, to deny to some people the fruits that "we" enjoy, but want to keep from "them." We need the game, the structured reminder of the dangers and of the possibilities. Watching the trailer for *Destiny*, I was reminded of the writings of St. John, who said in his gospel that it is given to us to become the sons of God (John 1:12), but even more of his first letter: "beloved, we are God's children now, but what we will be has not yet appeared" (John 3:2, English Standard Version). "It doesn't matter who you were; only what you will become."

Once, Dale described himself as a solitary, but now he just thinks of himself as an old guy living in the web and the Ozarks. More of his musings on the church year can be found at http://ringofthelord.blogspot.com.

The Tempter Came.
Tarah Van De Wiele

Who is shoeless and cold under all this makeup and costume?
Who was starving on Monday before this feast swept through our city?
I can't get beyond the questions, really
We clamour through the streets and toast to the revelry of Tuesday
But where are the clamberers for scraps to feed themselves in the morning?
Where have they gone?
On this night, they are swept beneath our sea of chaos let loose
Tonight's tambour and clamour drowns their steady song of every other day—
need upon need on play, repeating.

Everyone says it's a happy time tonight

We bask in the glow of our electric security from the darkness
Bathe in the affections that drunken strangers pour over our loneliness
Breathe in the immense power created when we paint our faces and dress like
gods.

Happy conquerors on a Tuesday

Happy to revel and live inside a human dream
Where security, esteem and power coat the world in a new wash of war paint
Hiding the endless expanse we feel between God and us
Such a coat seems to only ever last a night, of course
No matter how thickly layered on, by Wednesday morning we are lacklustre.

And Wednesday morning will always come

Who am I with just this ash on my face—no makeup, no costume?
Why am I still starving on Wednesday after this feast swept through our city?
I can't get beyond the questions, really
We shift through quiet streets and bear the ashes of Wednesday
Where is that sweet clamour to help me escape?
Where has it gone?
On this day, a bare wilderness appears for every soul under the sun instead
The silence burns away the tambour of the evening so we can hear
Burns away the paint so we can see

Everyone says it's impossible to follow him through this place

He does not bask in security, but runs into the darkness with only words
He does not bathe in affection, but covers himself in scorn and doubt
He does not breathe in power, but exhales a weakness called love

Defiant followers on a Wednesday

Defiant to follow him and live outside a human dream

Where trust, love and weakness expose the world and collapse the expanse
Shatter the illusion

Away with you! In the silence I hear the steady song
Away with you! Through these ashes I see the angels coming

Tarah is a theologian and biblical scholar living in Nottingham, UK with her husband and two dogs. When she is not buried neck-deep in studies, she speaks publically as ambassador and advocate for the Nottingham Arimathea Trust, which serves the physical, emotional and spiritual needs of destitute asylum seekers in the region.

Appendix A. Recipe Suggestions for Feasting

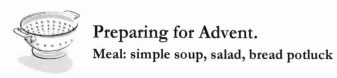

Preparing for Advent.
Meal: simple soup, salad, bread potluck

Yummy Yammy Stew
Ingredients: 1 Tbsp olive oil., 1 onion, chopped, 2 stalks celery, chopped, ½ bell pepper, chopped, 2 cloves garlic, chopped, 3 Cups vegetable broth, 3 Cups yams or sweet potatoes, cubed, 2 Cups diced tomatoes, 2 Cups cooked chickpeas, 1 Tbsp lemon juice, 2 tsp grated ginger, 1-2 tbsp each: cumin, curry powder, ground coriander (more as desired), 1 tsp chili powder, Salt & pepper to taste, 1/3 cup raisins, 3 Tbsp peanut butter, Handful of fresh cilantro, chopped

Instructions:

Sautee onions, celery, peppers, and garlic in olive oil until soft. Add rest of ingredients except raisins, nut butter and cilantro. Bring to boil. Reduce to simmer and cook, covered, for 20-30 minutes. Add raisins, nut butter and cilantro and simmer for 5 more minutes. Serve. Make 4-6 bowls.

—*Contributed by Michael Yankoski*

Cucumber/Avocado Salad:
Ingredients: Cucumber, Avocado, Olive Oil, Kosher Salt, Fresh Ground Pepper

Instructions: The quantity of cucumber and avocado are purely up to the salad maker! Add salt and pepper to taste.

—*Contributed by Cheryl Patz, chef-friend of Corean Bakke.*

Citrus Salad
Ingredients: 1 bag (or four hearts) of romaine, 1 avocado, 1 grapefruit, 1/3 cup feta cheese, 1/3 cup sliced almonds, 1/4 garlic vinaigrette (or dressing of choice)

Instructions: Tear lettuce leaves and top with sliced avocado, peeled grapefruit wedges, feta cheese and almonds. Toss with vinaigrette and enjoy!

Spinach Pistachio Salad
Ingredients: 1 bag of baby spinach, 1 carton of strawberries, 1/3 cup of shelled pistachios, 1/4 cup champagne vinegar, 1/4 cup olive oil, juice of one lime, pinch of cardamom, pinch of sea salt, 1 tablespoon of honey or agave nectar

Instructions: Mix the spinach with sliced strawberries and pistachios. In a separate bowl mix the champagne vinegar, honey or agave nectar, olive oil, lime juice, cardamom and sea salt. Toss together and enjoy!

—*Contributed by Monette Chilson*

Week One of Advent.
Meal: Mediterranean potluck

Papou's Greek Salad (Horiatiki)

Ingredients: 4 large, fresh and ripe tomatoes, 3 medium – large cucumbers, Approx. 1 lb. of feta cheese, 1 ½ c. of Kalamata olives, pits removed, Fresh or dried oregano to taste, Salt to taste, Olive oil

Instructions: Slice tomatoes into bite-size wedges. It's not necessary to discard the seeds. Slice cucumbers in half twice, so you have ½ moon-shaped slices. Mix these together in your serving bowl with the olives and enough live oil to coat the mix. Mix in enough oregano to lightly coat the ingredients. Add salt to taste. Slice the feta cheese in ¼ inch pieces and place them on top of the salad. Sprinkle more oregano on top of the feta. Serve immediately or chill for later use. Avoid putting olive oil on top of the feta as this will cause the cheese to fall apart.

—*Contributed by Joanna ES Campbell, who writes, "My father is a fan of all things Greek. His grandchildren call him Papou, which is a Greek endearment for grandpa. This is his recipe for Greek Salad, which he has been making for years and years.*

Spinach and Lemon Soup with Orzo (also known as Spinach Avgolemono) Serves 4-6

Ingredients: 2 tablespoons olive oil, 4 garlic cloves, smashed or minced, 1 large onion, 1 teaspoon red pepper flakes (or more, depending on your taste), 1 package frozen spinach, thawed and drained of excess water, 1 1/2 cups orzo, 8 cups chicken or vegetable broth, 4 eggs, Juice of 3 lemons, Fresh parsley, chopped (to serve) Fresh-grated Parmesan (to serve)

Instructions: Heat the olive oil in a large heavy pot or Dutch oven. Cook the garlic and onion over medium heat until fragrant and slightly translucent. Turn the heat to medium high and add the red pepper flakes, spinach, and orzo. Cook for about a minute, then add the broth. Bring to a light simmer, then turn the heat down and simmer for about 15 minutes, or until the orzo is just barely tender. Take the soup off the heat and let it cool down for a moment or two.

Whisk eggs vigorously in a largish bowl, then whisk in the lemon juice. Whisk for a couple minutes; the mixture should be thick, pale yellow, and creamy. Add a small ladleful of the soup broth to the eggs and whisk vigorously. (If you want to be really sure not to curdle the eggs, take a ladle of soup and cool it a bit before tempering the eggs.) Whisk in two more ladles of soup broth, whisking each well and letting them cool. Add the egg mixture to the soup pot, whisking very well. Return to very low heat, stirring the whole time. Cook carefully over low heat until the soup has thickened slightly. Serve immediately, garnished with parsley and Parmesan if desired.

—*Contributed by Karina Saunders, a resident of Mustard Seed House, who writes, "My oldest childhood friend is Greek. Her family owned an incredible Greek Restaurant in the West Village of NYC. Until it closed its doors Gus' Place was my favorite restaurant. The restaurant was full of love, from the warm whole wheat pita bread and delicious feta spread that met you when you sat in a candle-lit booth, to the fresh cut flowers arranged on each table by my friend's mom. Each detail at Gus' Place was well thought out and executed in love. Gus, my friend's father, knew his guests by name, and it was always a special treat when he would come and join your table for a few minutes to say "hi." One of my favorite dishes at Gus' Place was the* avgolemono, *a Greek lemon chicken soup. It was comfort food to me, and Gus would always have a special to-go order waiting for us if someone in the family came down with a cold.*

This recipe is not from Gus' Place, but when a friend sent it to me a few years ago the lemony egg soup quickly reminded me of childhood. Recipe adapted from: The Kitchen. http://www.thekitchn.com/recipe-spinach-and-lemon-soup-71789

Shakshuka [Eggs poached in spicy tomato sauce] serves 4-6

One of my favorite recipes is adapted from Deb Peralman's blog: Smitten Kitchen. *Shakshuka can be served as a brunch item or with rice or toasted flat bread for dinner. It's been a great last minute budget dinner and can easily serve a big group for a fellowship meeting. This dish taught me about the wonderful combination of tomatoes and eggs. Feel free to experiment with the ingredients and measurements; it doesn't need to be exact! Use what you have!*

Ingredients: 1/4 cup olive oil, 5 Anaheim chiles or 3 jalapeños, stemmed, seeded, and finely chopped, 1 small yellow onion, chopped, 5 cloves garlic, crushed then sliced, 1 teaspoon ground cumin, 1 tablespoon paprika, 1 28-ounce can whole peeled tomatoes, undrained, Kosher salt, to taste, 6 eggs, 1/2 cup feta cheese, crumbled, 1 tablespoon chopped flat-leaf parsley, Warm pitas, for serving.

Instructions: Heat oil in a 12-inch skillet over medium-high heat. Add chiles and onions and cook, stirring occasionally, until soft and golden brown, about 6 minutes. Add garlic, cumin, and paprika, and cook, stirring frequently, until garlic is soft, about 2 more minutes. Put tomatoes and their liquid into a medium bowl and crush with your hands. Add crushed tomatoes and their liquid to skillet along with 1/2 cup water, reduce heat to medium, and simmer, stirring occasionally, until thickened slightly, about 15 minutes. Season sauce with salt. Crack eggs over sauce so that eggs are evenly distributed across sauce's surface. Cover skillet and cook until yolks are just set, about 5 minutes. Using a spoon, baste the whites of the eggs with tomato mixture, being careful not to disturb the yolk. Sprinkle shakshuka with feta and parsley and serve with pitas, for dipping.

—*Contributed by Karina Saunders*

Week Two of Advent.
Meal: Southwestern foods potluck

Faux Molé Chili

A proper Mexican molé sauce begins with a preparation of dried peppers, and a standard sauce of this sort contains upward of 20 ingredients. As I usually have neither the time, ingredients, nor patience to prepare such a dish, I have developed a functional shortcut that makes a great bowl of chili from ingredients found in most pantries. My version relies on chocolate, cinnamon, chili powder, and a hefty splash of red wine to create a rich blend of flavors that is even better if left overnight before eating.

Ingredients: 1 lb ground beef, 1 medium onion, minced 2 cloves of garlic, minced, 1 Tbsp cocoa powder, 1 Tbsp ground cinnamon, 1 Tbsp chili powder, 1 tsp oregano, ¼ cup red wine, 1 14 oz. can tomato sauce, 1 6 oz. can tomato paste, 1 14 oz. can black beans, drained and rinsed, Cayenne pepper to taste

Instructions: Cook the ground beef and the onions together in a Dutch oven over medium heat until meat is browned and onions are translucent; add garlic about halfway through browning to prevent burning. Drain the beef mixture. Add spices, wine, tomato products, and beans. Bring to boil, then reduce to a simmer. Simmer on low for at least a half-hour. Serve with cornbread.

—*Contributed by Derek Olsen*

Tangy Chimichurri Sauce

Ingredients: 1 bunch flat leaf Italian Parsley, 2/3 cup dried oregano, 1 1/2 cup olive oil, 1/4 cup red wine vinegar, 3 cloves garlic, 1 tbs coarse sea salt, 1/2 tbs fresh ground pepper, 1 tsp red chili flakes

Instructions: Step 1: Combine all ingredients, except parsley, in a food processor or blender. If you do not have a food processor or blender available, chop finely and combine or grind in a pestle and mortar.

Step 2: Rinse and pat-dry parsley. Remove thick stems at the bottom, the thinner stems towards the leaves are ok. If using a food processor or blender, add parsley and pulse until parsley is chopped but not liquefied. If chopping or grinding in a pestle and mortar, parsley should be extremely small but still have some body to it.

Step 3: Let sit and combine for 1-2 hours so that oregano can soften and flavors can combine. Let stand overnight for best results.

Step 4: Serve with just about anything for an extra zing!

—Contributed by Katie Metzger, as shared on her blog www.samethread.com. *This is her husband, Nate's, recipe and is a staple in Argentina.*

Mesquite Chocolate Chip Cookies Recipe (Gluten Free)

For 2 dozen cookies: 1/2 c Mesquite flour, 1 1/2 c all-purpose flour (may substitute for gluten free), 1 t ground cinnamon, 1/4 c pecans or walnuts (optional), 1 c dark chocolate chips, 3/4 c softened butter, 3/4 c white sugar, 2 eggs

Instructions: Preheat oven to 375 degrees F (190 degrees C). Grease cookie sheets. Whisk together the mesquite flour, all-purpose flour, and cinnamon; set aside. Beat the butter and sugar with an electric mixer in a bowl until smooth. Add the eggs one at a time, allowing each egg to blend into the butter mixture before adding the next. Mix in the flour mixture until just incorporated. Drop by teaspoonfuls onto the prepared cookie sheets. Bake in the preheated oven until golden, 8 to 10 minutes. Remove from cookie sheets to cool on wire racks. Enjoy!

—Contributed by Maryada Vallet, who writes: It has become an annual tradition of mine to collect and mill Mesquite pods for desert-grown, golden delicious and naturally gluten-free flour. The pods dry up and fall from the scraggly native desert tree in the early summer, which is the key moment when the dedicated harvester collects a few buckets before the pods become drenched by the summer Monsoon rains. A local southern Arizona group then provides an

opportunity to mill the collected pods as a community event to celebrate native foods and the abundance of the Sonoran desertland that we call home. It is a leguminous food that has been enjoyed by the indigenous residents of the southwest for hundreds of years. This recipe is adapted from the following website, where non-desert dwellers may order Mesquite flour: http://store.casadefruta.com/mesquite-sale-c74.aspx.

Week Three of Advent.

Meal: Potluck of favorite family recipes

Great grandma's chicken n dumplings

Ingredients: 2 eggs, 1/2 cup chicken broth, 1/2 tsp baking powder, Pinch of salt, Flour

Directions: Mix in enough flour until slightly stiff, drop by teaspoon full into a large pot of boiling broth. They will float to the top very quickly. Then sprinkle in cooked shredded chicken. A warm hearty side dish or meal itself. This also works well with turkey

—Contributed by Kellie Carrara, passed down to her by her great grandmother

St. Lucia Bread

Pastry: 1/2 cup warm water (110-115), 2 packages active dry yeast 1-1 1/2 cups lukewarm milk, 1/2 cup sugar, 2 teaspoons salt, 2 eggs ½ cup soft shortening, 7 to 71/2 cups sifted all purpose flour, 1 teaspoon powdered saffron (if you do not have saffron, a few drops of yellow food coloring will do), raisins for decoration

Glaze: 1egg yolk, 1 tablespoon milk

Method: Dissolve saffron in 2 teaspoons boiling water. Strain if saffron is not powdered. Warm the milk over low heat. If the milk gets too hot, cool before using to avoid killing the yeast. Dissolve the yeast in warm water. Add the lukewarm milk, sugar, salt, 2 eggs, shortening, and half the flour. Add the dissolved saffron. Stir until smooth. Add the remaining flour a little at a time to make a dough which is easy to handle. You may or may not need all the flour. Mix the dough with, your hands. (or with a Kitchen Aid bread hook attachment) It is ready to knead when the dough stops sticking and pulls away from the bowl. Lightly flour your work surface. Knead until the dough is smooth and elastic, about 5 minutes or 200 turns. Place in a greased bowl. Cover and let rise in a warm place. About 1 1/2 hours. Punch dough down and allow to rise again. Roll out to 1/4 inch thickness, cut into strips 1/2 inch wide. Shape in traditional shapes. Let buns rise again (about 15-20 minutes) covered lightly with a clean towel. Brush with a glaze if desired. Bake at 400 for about 10 minutes or until golden brown

—*contributed by Mary Bergida, shared by her sister*

Week Four of Advent.

Meal: Cocoa, snacks, cookies, and appetizer potluck.

Hurry Up Hot Chocolate

Hot Chocolate is usually a spur-of-the-moment treat in our family, so this recipe has been honed through many years for simplicity, speed, and downright goodness. Read it once and you're ready to make it your own! This version is for two people, but it scales up easily. You will need **milk, salt, cocoa powder (fair trade if possible),** and **maple syrup**. (My stove is electric and takes a while to heat up – gas stoves may require some modification of this recipe.)

Put a saucepan over medium heat on the stove. Moving quickly, get two mugs and fill them with milk, then dump the milk into the saucepan, and place the mugs nearby. Next, get out cocoa powder, maple syrup and salt. Add a pinch of salt to the pan. Using a regular spoon from the silverware drawer, add three heaping spoons of cocoa to the saucepan. Using the same spoon, pour a steady stream of maple syrup over the spoon and into the pan, dumping the spoon each time it fills up until you've poured three spoons' worth (I call this three heaping spoons of maple syrup).

Here comes the best part: lick the spoon clean and set aside. Put away the cocoa, salt, maple syrup and milk, then quickly find a whisk and vigorously mix the saucepan's contents. The cocoa will resist your efforts, but the extra charge from cleaning the spoon should help you keep stirring. Once everything is smoothly mixed, check the temperature by sampling a spoonful. (Sometimes at this point I will add a bit of cinnamon and/or cayenne for extra flavor or top with whipped cream.) Stir occasionally until heated to taste, and then pour it into the mugs.

—*Contributed by Michael Carroccino*

Scottish Shortbread

Ingredients: 16 ounces butter, at room temperature, 2/3 cup sugar (in England or Australia use castor sugar), 1/2 cup rice flour, 3 1/2 cups all purpose flour

Method: 1. Cream butter and sugar until light and creamy. An electric mixer is best though I have also used a food processor. 2. Stir in sifted flours in 4 batches; when mixture becomes too stiff to stir, use hand to combine ingredients. 3. Turn on to lightly floured surface, knead lightly until smooth. 4. Scottish shortbread can be cooked in many ways. Here are some suggestions: Press mixture into a greased 11"x7" tin marked into squares or rectangles, prick with fork and bake in slow oven (150C or 300F) for 45 minutes, cut again into shapes stand 10 minutes in tin then remove and cool on wire rack.

Divide mixture into four parts. Shape each part into an eight inch round on a cookie sheet - 2 rounds should fit on each sheet. Decorate edge of round with the back of a fork, prick mixture with fork, bake in slow oven for 45 minutes. Cut each round into 8-12 wedges. Stand 10 minutes then remove and cool on wire rack. Press mixture into four wooden shortbread moulds which have been well rubbed with fingers dusted with cornflour (cornstarch). Cut away excess dough with a sharp knife, tap mould sharply on greased oven tray. Mould must be well rubbed with cornflour for each shortbread shape. Mixture will make 16 x 41/2" shapes. Cook in slow oven for 45 minutes. Stand for 10 minutes then lift onto a wire rack. Servings: 50

—*Contributed by Christine Sine, who writes, "This recipe was handed down to me by my mother who inherited it from her mother who was Scottish. My grandmother used arrowroot rather than rice flour. Traditionally Scottish shortbread is made for New Year's Eve (hogmanay) but I love to make it for Advent and the Christmas season.*

Kale Chips

1 bunch of kale, 2 tablespoons of olive oil, 2 tablespoons of Nama Shoyu or soy sauce,1/4 cup chia, flax or hemp seeds

Snip Kale off the stems with scissors or by hand. You want the kale in the largest piece possible because it will shrink significantly. Pour the olive oil and Nama Shoyu into the bowl and then throw the kale in. Toss with hands until all the leaves are coated, but not dripping. Lay kale leaves flat on a baking sheet lined with parchment paper and place them in a warming drawer on the medium setting (105 degrees) overnight or in the over at the lowest temperature setting for one to two hours. Check for crispness. You want to take them out when they are crisp like a chip.

—*Contributed by Monette Chilson*

New Year's Eve.

Meal: International foods potluck and/or cake and beverages at midnight

South Indian Chai (serves 2)

Put 1C milk 1C water in a saucepan.

Add 1-2 cardamom pods (ground in mortar/pestle, if possible)

Add 2 teaspoons of loose tealeaves.

Add 1/4 C. sugar. Bring to a boil. Boil until the mixture has a brown/tea color. Strain the bits. Serve hot.

Dum Byriani (serves 6)

Boil 3 C. jeera rice (or basmati) with mint leaves, salt, butter/ghee. Take cardamom, clove, cinnamon sticks and grind w/pestle and mortar. Add all, plus bay leaves to hot oil. Add 800 g onions to oil. Cook until brown. Add oil later if onions are not covered. Add 1 t. ginger/garlic paste. Cut 3 tomatoes. Add tomatoes. Add 1 C of fresh coconut. Add coriander, mint leaves, green chilies. (no red chilies) Add 1 kg chicken. (whole chicken, cut into pieces.) Cook chicken. Then, add 2 t. salt. When chicken is cooked, cover and let simmer for some time. (10 minutes). Put ghee/butter in LARGE pan. Combine rice mixture with gravy by layers. Rice, chicken, gravy. Add mint/coriander leaves. Repeat.

Both of these recipes were contributed by Andera Frankenfeld as taught to her by her friend Sanchita Robey when she lived in India.

Chocolate Pound Cake

Ingredients: 1 ½ C butter, 3 C sugar, 5 eggs, 3 C flour, ½ tsp. baking powder, 5 tbs. Cocoa (fair trade if possible), ½ tsp salt, 1 C milk, 2 tsp. vanilla

Directions: Cream butter while gradually adding sugar. Add eggs one at a time and beat. Sift together dry ingredients in a separate bowl, then alternate adding flour mixture and milk. Add vanilla. Bake 1 ½ hours at 325° in a greased and floured 10-inch tube pan.

—*Contributed by Michael Carroccino; Adapted from* Cotton Country Cooking, *a Junior League cookbook from Morgan County, Alabama.*

Twelfth Night.
Meal: Casserole potluck and king cake

Sweet Breakfast Casserole
The night before: Cut 8-10 slices of bread into cubes and arrange in the bottom of a greased 9x13 pan. Beat 8 eggs, 2 C. milk, 2 t. vanilla, cinnamon and ½ t. salt in a bowl. Pour over the bread. Cover the pan with plastic wrap and refrigerate overnight. Before baking: Melt ¾ C. butter in a saucepan. Add 1 1/3 C. brown sugar, ¼ C. maple syrup or honey, ½ t. vanilla and cinnamon. Heat on the stove (or in microwave) until sugar is melted and mixture is hot. Pour over the mixture in the pan. Bake at 350° for 30-40 minutes. Let stand 5 minutes (or more) before serving.
Contributed by Andrea Frankenfeld, who writes "Adapted from a recipe my friend DeLena Jones gave me."

St. Caedmon's Feast.
Meal: English potluck with ales or teas

Sun Tea
A gallon glass container filled with water,
Four licorice tea bags
Leave in the sun all day. Remove tea bags and refrigerate.
—Contributed by Corean Bakke, who writes, "This non-sugar drink is enjoyed by adults and children alike. I serve it as "Sun-Tea of the House."

Shepherd's Pie
Ingredients:
For mashed potatoes: 3-5 russet potatoes, peeled & cubed, 1/4 cup cream, 1 Tbsp butter, salt & ground pepper to taste
For filling: 1 Tbsp extra virgin olive oil, 1 Lb organic (grass fed optional) ground chuck roast or Lamb, pinch of salt, 1/2 tsp garlic, 1/2-1 onion diced, 1 cup chopped carrot, 3/4 cup frozen peas, 1/4 cup of sharp cheddar cheese, grated (optional)
For gravy: 2 Tbsp butter, 2 Tbsp flour, 1 cup beef stock or broth, 1 Tbsp Worcestershire sauce

Cooking Directions: Boil peeled & cubed potatoes until tender. Drain, pour into a bowl and add cream, butter, salt, and pepper. Mash potatoes until they are smooth (add cream if it is too dry). While potatoes boil, preheat a large skillet on medium heat. Add oil till hot, then beef or lamb, garlic and salt.

Brown and crumble the meat for 3-4 minutes. Add carrot and onion. Cook for another 5 minutes. Spoon meat and veggies from the skillet (leave drippings in pan). Turn to medium high heat and melt butter in the skillet. Whisk flour into room temperature stock or broth while butter is melting. Slowly pour broth/flour mixture into skillet and continuously stir with whisk. Add Worcestershire sauce. Continue stirring until gravy thickens. Reduce heat and stir meat and vegetable mixture into the gravy. Stir in peas. Transfer skillet contents into a large pie plate (or, if you are using an iron skillet, leave contents in the pan). Spoon mashed potatoes over meat, spread evenly. Place in preheated 350* oven for 20 minutes. Remove from oven and top with cheese. Heat under broiler for 1 minute.

—Contributed by Vera Miller, Kimberly Miller's mother. Their family lived in England when Kimberly was young. Shepherd's Pie is traditionally made with lamb or mutton.

Appendix B. More About the O Antiphons.

Sapientia-tide. *Derek Olsen*

I doubt you've heard of Sapientia-tide—but I'll bet you know "O Come, O Come Emmanuel." The liturgical obscurity and the popular hymn are both vestiges of an ancient tradition that celebrates the Incarnation of Christ: The Great "O" Antiphons. The intentional liturgical communities of the Middle Ages—the monastic houses and cathedrals—always sang the Song of Mary, the Magnificat, as part of their Evening Prayer (Vespers). To further their meditation upon the various mysteries of Christ made present in the liturgical cycles, one-line antiphons drawn from biblical or traditional sources were interwoven with Mary's canticle. The verses we now know as "O Come, O Come Emmanuel" are versions of the antiphons traditionally sung on the seven nights leading up to Christmas Eve. These antiphons are worthy of our attention as we enter this time before Christmas for both their spiritual riches and for their place in our Anglican heritage.

A curious entry appears in the December liturgical calendar of English Books of Common Prayer. The year 1561 brought an influx of minor saints from the Roman cycle back into the calendar of the Elizabethan Book of Common Prayer by way of the Latin Book of Common Prayer used in college chapels—places where Latin was expected to be "a tongue understanded of the people." But among this number came an entry that was not the name of a saint or martyr. December 16th bears the legend: O Sapientia—O Wisdom. Formally ratified by its inclusion in the calendar of the 1662 Prayer Book—still the official prayer-book of the Church of England and often considered the liturgical norm for the Anglican Communion—this entry holds an indisputable place in our history grounding the "O" Antiphons in the Anglican tradition although they have never yet appeared in an official prayer book. (The Church of England's *Common Worship* does include a version, though.) The Roman Catholic Church has retained these antiphons as well, but their course begins on December 17th—meaning that the Anglican tradition retains an antiphon no longer used by Rome. Ironically, the missing antiphon is the one addressed to the Blessed Virgin Mary.

Jumping back a thousand years, the deep roots of the antiphons in the English tradition may be seen in the leaves of the Exeter Book, a collection of poetic texts and riddles from the tenth century written in Old English. The opening lines—only partially preserved—are poetic paraphrases of not seven but twelve "O" antiphons that ponder the Advent, the time of waiting, the Incarnation, and its implications for fallen humanity. The choice of these antiphons are a starting place for deep meditations on God and humanity is not happenstance—rather these texts are rich with spiritual and doctrinal content that beg for further expansion, explanation, and appreciation. I feel this urge today as surely as it was felt over a millennium ago.

The antiphons are a mosaic of Scriptural citations and allusions. As Advent privileges the writings of the prophets, so the central image of each antiphon is drawn from a prophet nugget. Since the Book of Revelation was composed in a similar fashion—always in conversation with the prophets and the psalms—many of the prophetic nuggets have picked up an unearthly sheen from John's words as well. We hear the words of the prophets not only from their own time and place but through the lens of New Testament's use of them. In the scriptural cloud that surrounds each core image, some links are obvious—others are less so, drawing on the interpretive methods and decisions of the Church Fathers.

Each antiphon begins with a metaphor, a title for Christ, most evoking not just a passage but whole swathes of Scripture. This metaphor is expanded by ancillary images and references that add depth and dimension to the Scriptural stories. Last, an imperative beseeches Christ to come and liberate us from sin, death, and darkness. As we take the words and images of the prophets in our mouths, we join their cry for the coming of the babe of Bethlehem. And speaking our own future, we call for the Coming King who will consummate the redemption of all creation. And—furthermore—we cry Christ into our own hearts, asking that the birth of the divine child be not only in history of distant days or future consummation but that we see, we experience, his redemptive resurrection power in our own flesh.

Dec 17th:[46] O Wisdom that comest out of the mouth of the Most High, that reachest from one end [of the heavens] to another, and dost mightily and sweetly order all things: come to teach us the way of prudence!

Dec 18th: O Adonai, and Ruler of the house of Israel, who didst appear unto Moses in the burning bush, and gavest him the law in Sinai: come to redeem us with outstretched arm!

---

[46] English texts from the public domain The Roman Breviary, translated by John, Marquis of Bute (Edinburgh: Blackwood, 1908,) 244.

Dec 19th: O Root of Jesse, which standest for an ensign of the people, at whom the kings shall shut their mouths, unto whom the Gentiles shall seek: come to deliver us, make no tarrying!

Dec 20th: O Key of Davd and Sceptre of the house of Israel; that openest and no man shutteth; and shuttest and no man openeth: come to bring out the prisoners from the prison, and them that sit in darkness, and in the shadow of death!

Dec 21st: O Day-spring Brightness of the everlasting Light, Sun of Righteousness: come to give light to them that sit in darkness, and in the shadow of death!

Dec 22nd: O King of the Gentiles, yea, and Desire thereof, O Cornerstone that makest of twain [two] one: come to save man, whom Thou hast made of the dust of the earth!

Dec 23rd: O Emmanuel, our King and our Law-giver, Longing of the Gentiles, yea, and Salvation thereof: come to save us, O Lord our God!

(If the missing optional antiphon is used, it should be used on the 23rd and the others moved back one day: O Virgin of Virgins, how shall this be? For neither before thee was any like thee, nor shall there be after. Daughters of Jerusalem, why marvel ye at me? That which ye behold is a divine mystery.)

Derek Olsen is a layperson in the Diocese of Maryland where his wife is a priest and his daughters are an acolyte and boat-bearer respectively. He received a Ph.D. in New Testament from Emory University and his research focuses on the intersection between Scripture and Liturgy. He serves as Secretary of the Standing Commission on Liturgy & Music and is the Liturgical Editor of the newly revised edition of the Saint Augustine's Prayer Book. *An IT specialist by day, Derek created and maintains the online Daily Office site* The St. Bede's Breviary. *His reflections on life, Anglo-Catholic identity, and liturgical spirituality appear at* Haligweorc.

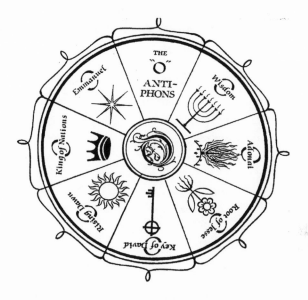

O Antiphon Symbols used by St. Mark's Episcopal Cathedral, Seattle, Washington.

O Antiphon Program Notes.
Peter Hallock

Program Notes by Peter Hallock from the cd booklet:
An Advent Procession: Based on the Great "O" Antiphons
The Choirs of St. Mark's Cathedral - Seattle, Washington

For more than fifty years, special evening celebrations on the First Sunday of Advent have been important events in the liturgical life of St. Mark's Cathedral, Seattle. The format of these services has followed the tried and true formula of readings from scripture with a variety of musical responses: processionals, psalms, carols, anthems and hymns.

That such a reasonable format should eventually suggest other possibilities did not arise until the use of that format (i.e. Lessons and Carols a la King's College, Cambridge) seemed, not only in its redundancy, but also in its singular association with Christmas, to confuse and negate the distinctions appropriate to these important celebrations of Advent. Thus the question, "what to do?"

Thanks to an opportunity for creative dialogue with Dr. William Bertolas, at that time a member of the Compline Choir, we investigated the potential that seemed inherent in the Gregorian Chant settings of the Great "O" Antiphons, which have languished for too long on the dusty back shelves of liturgical disuse. While Christians of numerous denominations have for many years been singing the "O" Antiphons in the form of the hymn O come, O come, Emmanuel it seemed likely that this practice in itself had not really brought to life the vibrant images of Christ drawn from the Old Testament: Wisdom, Adonai, Root of Jesse, Key of David, Rising Dawn, King of Nations, and Emmanuel. Thus to celebrate the beginning for the Advent seasons with a liturgy in which the power of these images might be more vividly displayed and discovered anew became our goal.

The shape of the liturgy is quite simple: banners displaying the symbols of each antiphon are brought from the rear of the church, one at a time, as each antiphon is sung. After each banner is placed in the chancel a reading from scripture, a musical response (congregational hymn, carol or motet) and a prayer are offered. As a final musical response the hymn Veni, veni Emmanuel is sung with all of the banners carried in a grand exit procession.

Involved in the preparation of the first "O" Antiphon liturgy at St. Mark's were the following: the officiant, thurifer, seven readers, the Cathedral Choir, the Compline Choir, the organist, seven acolytes to carry banners, seven torchbearers to precede each banner in the procession. Various choir members and friends made the banners and the wooden stands that held the banners in the chancel. The generous hands on help of two members of the Altar Guild were of invaluable assistance in dealing with candles and innumerable back-stage details essential to successful execution of such an elaborate liturgy.

Few liturgies offer the opportunity for such wide and diverse participation of the laity, both in preparation and execution. It is from this standpoint that I feel those who prepare and offer this liturgy will find their greatest rewards and satisfaction.

—Peter Hallock

Peter Hallock, November 19, 1924-April 27, 2014, was an organist, composer, choirmaster, liturgist, and founding director of the Compline Choir at St. Mark's Episcopal Cathedral in Seattle.

Appendix C. More About French Santons (Nativity Figures)

Santons and Their Christmas Lessons.
Barbara Beckwith

Santons are, literally, "little saints." Part of a typical French Nöel crèche (Christmas Nativity scene), santons come in work clothes to visit the Holy Family. They bring the Christ Child presents they have made or grown, hunted or sold. They perform or offer simple gestures of thoughtfulness.

Santons may have inspired St. Francis to re-create the scene of Jesus' birth at Greccio in 1223, usually given credit for ushering in the tradition of Christmas crèches. Some think that Lady Pica, Francis' mother, may have brought an early

Nativity set with her from Beaucaire (or Tarascon) in France when she married Lombard merchant Pietro and moved to Assisi.

Provençal santon figures are delightfully anachronistic: They do not portray people of Jesus' day, but rather typical characters of an 18th- or 19th-century village in France.

Origins of the Tradition

The santon tradition began with small figures of wood or wax or clay that were traded around the Mediterranean, possibly originating in Naples (which went on to develop its presepios). Santons existed in the 13th century, in the provinces of the Midi and along the banks of the Rhône River. The French kept developing the figures in a unique way.

In 1803, French craftspeople started a Nativity fair at Marseilles to display and sell their work. The fair's success spurred artisans to create more figures of ordinary people involved in the Christmas story, figures of local interest, with familiar faces and occupations. The fair has continued, with santon makers setting up stalls along the Canebière every Advent through Epiphany.

But santons are not merely a merchandising success; they were a way of bringing religion home and keeping it alive in the wake of the French

Revolution of 1789. When churches were being sacked, looted and closed, and Christmas Midnight Mass and outdoor Nativity scenes were banned, ordinary people began setting up crèches in their own homes, a tradition previously reserved for the rich. These displays became more and more elaborate, as the whole social structure of a Provençal village was recreated.

Village Life

Typical of all crèches, a Provençal Nativity scene begins with the Holy Family (although the Virgin Mary, St. Joseph, Jesus, the Three Kings and the angels are not technically santons).Vierge Marie (Mary) wears blue and white garments as a symbol of her purity. Sant Jòusè (Joseph) is dressed in a traveling cloak and often carries a staff. Jésus, blond, fair-skinned and pink-cheeked, is wrapped in a simple piece of cloth and lying on straw, an image of innocence but also l'Enfant-roi (Child-King). (The whiteness of the child is not so much to designate his race as to denote his kingliness.)

The Rois Mages (the Three Wise Men) are powerful, wise and learned. Their robes may be decorated with the fleur-de-lis, a lily associated with royalty. The kings may be accompanied by a one-humped camel and a camel driver, the servant of the kings. The story goes that, after being baptized by St. Thomas, they returned to spread the gospel to their own people.

There are angels, of course. The standing angel gives the message of Jesus' birth; the herald angel guides people to Jesus with his trumpet; cherubim watch over the newborn Jesus. The angels' message comes not to the shepherds of Bethlehem but to the shepherds of Provence, depicted in various poses.

The pastor of St. Anthony of Padua Parish in Manchester, New Hampshire, Father Charles DesRuisseaux, has a santon collection displayed annually at the diocesan museum. He's collected the stories that go with the figures. One concerns the shepherd Gabriel whose dog has just died. Gabriel thinks he is too sad to go to see the newborn Jesus, because "it would not be right to go to such a joyous event with tears in my eyes." But then his dog gets up as if he had only been sleeping. Gabriel decides to give the dog to Jesus as a present, but Mary tells him, "No, thank you. Keep your beautiful dog. You need him more than we do. My Son will someday be a shepherd, too, a shepherd of people, and for that he does not need a dog."

The shepherds summon all Provençal villagers. They bring their unique gifts to honor the newborn child: the baker (or his son) with typical Provençal breads like la banette and le pain Calendal (a round country loaf marked with a cross and baked only at Christmastime), the vegetable merchant, the cheese vendor, the basket maker, the wine grower, the humble woman or man who brings only a bundle of sticks for a fire to keep the baby warm.

A poor old man, who thinks he has nothing to give the Baby, holds his lantern and offers to light the way for others. His gift of thoughtfulness and courtesy earns him a place in the scene.

Santons come from all occupations and show typical French customs: the fisherman with his nets and his wife who sells the fish and weighs them on her scales, a woman with a pot of snails (a traditional French delicacy) or another housewife fattening a goose for foie gras, the farmer and his pig with the long snout searching for truffles, the mayor in his frock coat, the midwife with her cradle, the parish priest (Monsieur le Curé) and the monk in cowled habit. All classes of society, all ages of people, are represented.

The grandmother is knitting socks for l'Enfant Jésus. The flower seller has a bouquet for Jesus. The woman with the chicken is offering it for soup, traditionally made for new mothers to recover their strength. The soap peddlers bring the Marseilles soap made of olive oil and soda ash; after their travels, the Holy Family would have appreciated soap. There is even a santon wet nurse for the Baby so that Mary can have a nap.

There's a swarthy Gypsy woman who carries a baby and tambourine to provide music for Jesus, and a Gypsy man who brings his bear to perform. The fact that Gypsies, outsiders often despised as chicken thieves, were included in crèche scenes says something about even ordinary people realizing how far the Incarnation and redemption extend.

A legend recounted by Father DesRuisseaux involves the Gypsy Séraphin who hears the Angel Boufarèu ("Big Cheeks") blow his trumpet to an-nounce that le Bon Dieu (the Good God) "has become a daddy." For the first time in his life, Séraphin feels guilty for stealing. He tries to give Mary the stolen chicken and eggs, but Mary tells him, "I realize you have a big heart, but my Son would prefer that you give them back to their owner." That story ends, "From that day, the Gypsy never stole again."

Typical santon scenes include musicians and dancers who dance the farandole with joined hands.

The stories of some santon figures come from legends and plays. The old man (Roustido) heard the shepherds' call late and tried to awaken his neighbors, Monsieur Jordan and Margarido (who rides a donkey). Roustido is doffing his nightcap in greeting to the Holy Family. A brave and simple farmhand (Pistachié) falls into a well trying to draw water for Margarido's donkey.

A typical santon scene includes various animals beyond the traditional ox and the ass: sheepdogs with bells under their necks, as well as sheep; brown, gray and white goats, rabbits lying down or standing up, pigeons on the roof, and other barnyard animals.

Other regions of France, like Brittany, Normandy and Alsace, developed figures unique to them. (Catalonia, Spain, developed figures, too.) French immigrants to Québec, Canada, brought the santon tradition with them; the area around Charlevoix has developed santons of fur traders.

The ravi is an important Provençal santon, according to Betsy Christensen, an avid American santon collector from Ann Arbor, Michigan, who spent time in France when her husband was teaching there. The ravi or ravie is a man or woman in rapture, always portrayed with arms upraised.

There are also men and women on their knees praying. Such stories prompt us to ask, "What is my response to Jesus' coming?"

Made of Clay

There are two types of Provençal santons: santons d'argile (hand-painted clay figures) and santons habilles (figures dressed in real cloth and carrying actual baskets, lavender, fishing nets and so on).

The clay figures come in six sizes (from one inch to six inches tall). The dressed figures range from six inches to 18 inches tall.

Nowadays, santons are never made of plastic, lead or plaster, but always clay. (The insistence on clay seems appropriate since Genesis 2:7 says that the Lord God used clay to form the first human. Was God a santon maker?) The clay for santons comes from quarries near Marseilles and Aubagne.

Molds are created from which between 200 and 1,000 copies can be made. Most contemporary santons are fired in kilns for 48 hours at 1,650° F. The subsequent painting is done in small quantities due to the drying time necessary between colors. A base coat is put on first, then all the greens, the blues and so on.

The Theological Message

Santons are a natural way of doing catechesis with children, just as crib scenes are used by some American families. That the figures can be touched, dressed, decorated and loved like dolls is an advantage in teaching children. They are small and fit children's hands. Having parents repeat year after year the legends about particular santons is a friendly way of teaching and makes the stories a beloved holiday tradition.

In November, Provençal families get the cardboard boxes with the figures out of the cupboard and begin to arrange the buildings, scenes and cast of characters. An expedition to the country to obtain new moss, leaves and bits of wood may be necessary. New figures may be purchased at the santon fairs—new ones are developed yearly. This year's Christmas scene may need a pigeon roost or a bridge. Lots of imagination goes into arranging the scene.

In Woolwich, Maine, Betsy (who uses only her first name professionally) says that, before becoming the owner of Santons de France USA, her family had a santon tradition: "On Thanksgiving Eve we would gather our five children around a box filled with individually wrapped santon figures. Taking turns, each child would open the wrapping, revealing the figure, and place it around the stable. I highly recommend this enjoyable tradition. Watch their eyes light up when the lucky child opens the Baby Jesus." This tradition is now in its fourth generation in her family.

During Advent the santon figures may be moved around a bit to convey that this is an ongoing story. Special Advent sets of Mary (astride a donkey) and Joseph with a walking staff can be moved closer to the stable each day. The Baby Jesus can be placed just before Christmas Midnight Mass. The Three Kings can draw nearer daily until they arrive on Epiphany.

This kind of ritual can prepare us for Christmas. "The santons provide the chance for ordinary folk to compose Nativity scenes akin to those previously reserved only for the rich," according to The Little Dictionary of Santons de Provence, prepared by Marcel Carbonel's studios.

Carbonel, who died in 2003 at the age of 93, created a hundred or more crib figures over 50 years. His company in Marseilles and that of Paul Fouque's in Aix-en-Provence are the largest of the 60 santon-making companies in France.

Santons and their stories "will continue as long as there remains a desire to put on stage those timeless, mythical characters, symbols of dreams and mystery yet representing the realities of everyday life," predicted Carbonel.

All of Life Can Be Holy

Santons underscore the fact that Jesus came to participate in our everyday life. That our God should worry about snails and garlic is part of the wondrous mystery of the Incarnation. And santons teach us that it is through our occupations and roles in life that we come to him and complete our redemption begun at Christmas.

Composing the Nativity story for ourselves and our families is the heart of the santon theology. We must tell the story of Jesus' birth and life and death in the way we understand it. And we must put ourselves in the story because Jesus came to earth for us just as much as the first-century Holy Land residents.

According to Father DesRuisseaux, usually the parents in Provence conclude the santon stories told to their children this way: "After the people of Bethlehem had brought their best gifts to the Christ Child, in gratitude to the Good God who had made little miracles to better their lives, they were turned into statues. Now we take them out every year to display in our Nativity scenes to remind us that, on that first Christmas, the Good God gave us the best gift ever—his Son, Jesus Christ."

Santons idealize a pastoral lifestyle and celebrate a particular slice of life. But by doing so, santons remind us that Jesus is born into every culture and every time. Christmas is our story and we, too, can be "little saints" coming to present our gifts to the Christ Child.

The national organization Friends of the Creche had presentations about santons at its 2002 meeting by Betsy Christensen and its 2003 convention by Father Charles DesRuisseaux. (www.udayton.edu/mary/gallery/creches/crechefriends.html) To join and/or sign up for their newsletter contained in the publication Creche Herald (www.op.net/~bocassoc), write: Editor Rita Bocher.

"Santons and Their Christmas Lessons" by Barbara Beckwith, from St. Anthony Messenger *magazine, is used by permission of Franciscan Media, 28 W. Liberty St., Cincinnati, OH 45202.* www.FranciscanMedia.org. ©2004.

Photo by Daniel Ferrier, Wikipedia Commons

More About Mustard Seed Associates

"He told them another parable: 'The kingdom of heaven is like a mustard seed, which a man took and planted in his field...'" (Matthew 13:31).

The Mustard Seed Associates team seeks to enable followers of Jesus—especially those who are innovators and unsatisfied with 'status quo' faith—to a countercultural way of life. We encourage people to create new and innovative forms of whole life faith that advance God's purposes locally and globally and engage tomorrow's challenges. We want to create processes and offer resources that ignite people's creativity and inspire them to live as agents of faith—a faith that is more culturally subversive and revolutionary than we can fully understand or imagine.

Additional MSA Resources

Publications

A Journey into Wholeness: Soul Travel from Lent to Easter, compiled by Christine Sine, Kristin Carroccino, and Ricci Kilmer

Waiting for the Light: An Advent Devotional, compiled by Susan Wade, Ricci Kilmer, and Christine Sine

Return to Our Senses: Reimagining How We Pray, by Christine Sine

To Garden with God, by Christine Sine

To Garden with God: Color Edition, by Christine Sine

Light for the Journey: Morning and Evening Prayers for Living into God's Word, by Christine Sine

GodSpace: Time for Peace in the Rhythms of Life, by Christine Sine

Living On Purpose: Finding God's Best for Your Life, by Christine and Tom Sine

The New Conspirators, by Tom Sine

E-Books

Celebrating the Joy of Easter, by Christine Sine

Turbulent Times, Ready or Not!, by Tom Sine

Shalom and the Wholeness of God, by Christine Sine

Justice at the Table, by Ricci Kilmer

To Garden With God (.PDF, .MOBI, .ePUB Versions)

Waiting for the Light: An Advent Devotional (PDF and Kindle Versions)

A Journey into Wholeness: a Lenten Journey (PDF Version)

E-Course

Reimagining How We Pray

Other Resources

Prayer Cards

Gardener's Soap

All resources (including video and audio resources, tickets to MSA events, study guides and links to blogs) may be accessed and ordered at http://msaimagine.org/resources.

A free resource guide of many more ideas for observing the seasons of Advent to Lent is available at msaimagine.org under the "Resources" tab. Please visit *Godspace* to enjoy ongoing contributions from writers throughout the year.

Acknowledgments

I would like to thank all of the contributors to *A Journey toward Home*; without each of them, this journey would have been lonely! Jen Loser, thanks for your help in finishing the collage for the cover art and for the inspiring conversation about being artists. Many thanks to Mary Ratcliffe, who assisted in the final proofreading of the manuscript from afar, Danielle Poland for designing the O Antiphon icons, and Karina Saunders for last minute recipe inspiration. The Mustard Seed Associates team is always an inspiration for growing big ideas from tiny mustard seeds into reality; thanks especially to Andy Wade and, of course, Christine Sine. Without Christine's hard work for, and commitment to, MSA, resources like this one wouldn't exist. No book would ever be written without patience, love, and "creative" scheduling on the part of family and best friends, so for their generosity and kindness thanks to Michael, Caedmon, and Mirella.

—Kristin

I love seeing the posts contributed to *Godspace* come together in a book like this, and am grateful for each author who has added their inspiring words to its content. Unfortunately, there are too many to name! I am also thankful for the artistic talent of Danielle Poland, whose O Antiphon icons so enrich the presentation. So many others have come alongside to help bring this book to completion: Mary Ratcliffe, who provided editorial advice, and the MSA team— Andy Wade, Katie Metzger and Tom Sine. I am grateful for the ways that all of you have gone the extra mile to help us finish this project. Most of all I am grateful to my co-author, Kristin Carroccino, who has worked tirelessly for many months to bring this project to completion, encouraging me to continue when I was ready to give up. Without her and her husband Michael, this book would never have come into being. Thank you from the bottom of my heart.

—Christine

About Kristin Carroccino and Christine Sine

Kristin Carroccino is a writer and artist currently living in Seattle. She is a contributor to and editor of several books, including this one as well as *A Journey Into Wholeness: Soul Travel from Lent to Easter*, both publications of Mustard Seed Associates. Her poetry has been published in several small journals. She enjoys teaching her son and daughter all sorts of interesting things, especially natural history and mindfulness techniques. She is learning a lot about robotics from her son and how to build fairy houses and trap Leprechauns with her daughter. She experiences the movement of Spirit most often in nature, listening to beautiful music and prayers, and reading complicated poetry and prose on the couch under a blanket with a mug of tea.

Christine Sine is the Executive Director of Mustard Seed Associates. She describes herself as a contemplative activist and is passionate about helping people connect their spiritual practices to their everyday life. She conducts workshops and retreats that help participants develop more spiritual rhythms. Christine is also the author of several books, the latest being *To Garden with God* and *Return to Our Senses: Reimagining How We Pray*. Christine blogs at *http://godspace-msa.com*. You can follow her on twitter at *https://twitter.com/ChristineSine*, or read her daily prayers posted on the *Light for the Journey* Facebook page: *https://www.facebook.com/pages/Light-for-the-Journey/*.

Made in the USA
Charleston, SC
15 November 2014